Lysistrata

Other Wisconsin Studies in Classics works by
DAVID MULROY

The Complete Poetry of Catullus
Catullus; translated and with commentary

Oedipus Rex
Sophocles; a verse translation, with introduction and notes

Antigone
Sophocles; a verse translation, with introduction and notes

Oedipus at Colonus
Sophocles; a verse translation, with introduction and notes

Agamemnon
Aeschylus; a verse translation, with introduction and notes

*The Oresteia: "Agamemnon," "Libation Bearers," and
"The Holy Goddesses"*
Aeschylus; a verse translation, with introduction and notes

Lysistrata

A New Verse Translation

Aristophanes

Translated by David Mulroy

THE UNIVERSITY OF WISCONSIN PRESS

Publication of this volume has been made possible, in part, through the generous support and enduring vision of Warren G. Moon.

The University of Wisconsin Press
728 State Street, Suite 443
Madison, Wisconsin 53706
uwpress.wisc.edu

Gray's Inn House, 127 Clerkenwell Road
London EC1R 5DB, United Kingdom
eurospanbookstore.com

Printed in the United States of America
This book may be available in a digital edition.

Library of Congress Cataloging-in-Publication Data
Names: Aristophanes, author. | Mulroy, David D., 1943– translator.
Title: Lysistrata : a new verse translation / Aristophanes ;
translated by David Mulroy.
Other titles: Lysistrata. English (Mulroy)
Description: Madison, Wisconsin : The University of Wisconsin Press, [2020]
Identifiers: LCCN 2020016437 | ISBN 9780299329846 (paperback)
Subjects: LCSH: Lysistrata (Fictitious character)—Drama. | Greece—History—Peloponnesian War, 431–404 B.C.—Drama. | LCGFT: Drama.
Classification: LCC PA3877 .L8 2020 | DDC 882/.01—dc23
LC record available at https://lccn.loc.gov/2020016437

In loving memory of
Mary Joyce Mulroy, née Donnelly (1943–2020)

"The Iliad must lose a lot in the original Greek."

Contents

Introduction

Lysistrata is one of the best-known and most-loved ancient Greek comedies. It is a whimsical fantasy composed midcareer by Aristophanes, the leading exponent of ancient Greek comedy. In it, an Athenian woman, Lysistrata by name, brings peace to Greece by persuading its women to withhold sexual favors from their warring husbands until they resolve their differences—which they quickly do.

Much of Aristophanes' humor is topical. Allusions to real persons and events abound. Knowledge of general historical circumstances is taken for granted. In view of all that, I devote much of the introduction to a sketch of relevant Athenian history and pay special attention to events alluded to in the play. Such material could be, and in some cases has been, relegated to notes, but some of it benefits from a more detailed narration.

My description of *Lysistrata*'s historical background is followed by a synopsis of the play itself. It is intended to help readers who are unfamiliar with Aristophanes' works, which seem chaotic on first reading.

I add a brief summary of what little is known of Aristophanes' private life, the highlights of his career as a poet, and some notes concerning pronunciation and related matters.

Two appendices follow the play's text: a pronunciation guide and a description of the meters I have employed in translation.

Historical Background

Greece of the sixth and fifth centuries BCE was a collection of independent city-states, each with its own laws and customs. For many of those states, the great challenge was the suppression of class warfare. In Athens that problem was addressed with some success by the poetry and legislative reforms of Solon, who was tasked with reforming Athenian laws at the beginning of the sixth century. His reforms were aimed at achieving a compromise between the demands of the rich and those of the poor. In the end, he satisfied neither. Tensions rose until a strongman emerged by the name Pisistratus.

Pisistratus used various clever stratagems to gain power in Athens. For example, he staged an attack against himself and then persuaded the assembly[1] to grant him a bodyguard, which he proceeded to use for his own ends. This was just the first of three attempts by Pisistratus to install himself as the de facto ruler of Athens. The third attempt, for which he raised a small army, was successful. Athens flourished under the rule of the "tyrant"[2] Pisistratus from 547 BCE until his death in 527 BCE. He was succeeded by his son, Hippias, who was exiled in 510 BCE.

The story behind that involves Hippias' brother, Hipparchus, and two Athenian nobles: the handsome youth Harmodius and his middle-aged lover Aristogeiton. Hipparchus fell in love with Harmodius, but that youth—being true to Aristogeiton—rejected

Hipparchus' advances. Viewing this as a deadly insult, Hipparchus got even by having Harmodius' sister declared unfit to march in a religious procession. In turn, Harmodius and Aristogeiton were so angry that they felt compelled to assassinate Hippias and Hipparchus, and they recruited a number of disaffected nobles to help. They planned to strike at the Panathenaea,[3] at a given signal, but the plot misfired. One of the would-be assassins was seen talking to Hippias. This caused Harmodius and Aristogeiton to panic and attack and kill Hipparchus before the conspirators were in a position to help. At the far end of the procession, Hippias was advised of the event. He immediately had the soldiers with him searched. In some accounts, they all carried twigs of myrtle, gifts for Athena. The conspirators also used their twigs to conceal daggers. This enabled Hippias to identify, arrest, and punish the conspirators. At the head of the procession, Harmodius and Aristogeiton were also seized and killed.

As time passed, the Athenians took increasing pride in the democratic constitution that eventually—after another struggle—replaced Pisistratid rule. Politicians excited their supporters by accusing their opponents of plotting to overthrow the democracy and replace it with a tyranny. As memories dimmed, the Athenians falsely credited Harmodius and Aristogeiton with being responsible for restoring liberty to Athens. In a few years, a statue of "The Tyrannicides," with daggers bared, was proudly displayed in the Athenian marketplace.

Aristophanes makes fun of all this in *Lysistrata*. His male choristers are all senior citizens. They would have to have been over a hundred to take part in the assassination of Hipparchus. That does not prevent them from feeling as though they are standing at Aristogeiton's side as they prepare to confront the women of Athens. They know what the women are up to.

Clearly what they're weaving now's a cloak for tyranny
Never shall a gang of tyrants get the best of me!
I've unsheathed my dagger, which these myrtle blossoms hide
while I stand in armor at Aristogeiton's side . . .
strike a noble pose like so, then leaping from my place,
smash that ancient, god-forsaken woman's ugly face.

(630–635)

In fact, Hippias was a mild ruler before his brother's assassination. Afterwards, he became fearful and had citizens killed or exiled from the fear of similar plots.

An initial attempt to drive Hippias out of Athens was led by a rich, influential clan known as the Alcmaeonids. They occupied a fortress named Leipsydrium on the outskirts of Athenian territory, hoping to make it their base of operations, but were driven out of it in short order by Hippias' men.

It is not known how well the Alcmaeonids fought before they were driven out. Whether weak or strong, their resistance was celebrated for over a century in songs sung at banquets. Aristotle (*Constitution of the Athenians* 19.3) preserves an example:

Traitorous Leipsydrium!
Friendly hill of deadly fame!
Your victims showed the virtue of
the fathers whence they came.

Aristophanes' choristers also think of them as models of courage:

Yo white-footed men
who stormed Leipsydrium

when we were still a thing,
the time to rise has come.

We have to fly again
and shake our bodies free
from head to toe of all
of age's misery.
                    (664–670)

In fact, there is no evidence that the rebels who occupied Leipsy-drium had to fight for it. It is just as likely that they took up resi-dence there when it was unoccupied and did not fight at all until they were forced out. It is not known why they are called white-footed. Perhaps they endured a snowstorm while camping out on Leipsydrium.

Later the Spartans decided to help the Athenian exiles defeat Hippias. An initial attempt failed because Hippias had the help of allies, cavalry men from Thessaly (northern Greece). The second attempt, however, led to victory for the Athenian exiles. This time, the Spartan contingent was led by King Cleomenes himself. Hippias and his family surrendered without a fight when their children were captured as they were being led away to safety.

In 510 BCE, the Athenians were free of tyranny thanks to—of all people—the Spartans. Lysistrata stresses the point in mak-ing the case for peace to the Athenian chorus. She maintains that the expulsion of Hippias also rescued the Athenians from dire poverty—a more doubtful assertion:

Remember how the Spartans rescued you
when you were dressed in wooly peasant frocks?

They killed a thousand men of Thessaly
together with the friends of Hippias.
They cast them out alone that happy day
and freed the state. Instead of wooly frocks,
you started wearing finely woven robes.

(1150–1156)

In fact, no less an authority than Aristotle (*Constitution of the Athenians* 16.7) writes that the reign of the Pisistratids was a period of peace and prosperity.

In 508 BCE, the choice for the highest magistracy in Athens lay between an oligarch,[4] Isagoras, and a "champion of the people," Cleisthenes the Alcmaeonid. Isagoras won the election, but Cleisthenes and his supporters overturned the result with mass protests. The Spartans didn't like tyrants, but they were fond of oligarchs. They dispatched Cleomenes and a small band of soldiers to Athens to restore Isagoras. Instead, the Athenian commoners rose up and laid siege to the Spartans and Isagoras in the Acropolis until they abandoned their opposition to Cleisthenes and his reforms.

In the play, the men's chorus looks back fondly on this humiliation of a Spartan king.

We guarantee these women won't
    be laughing any longer!
Cleomenes, a king no less,
    once occupied the Polis.
He didn't leave triumphant though
    he claimed to be a Spartan!

He gave up shield and weapons
    walking down surrender's path

and looked a mess, as though he'd gone
  six years without a bath.

$$(271–280)$$

In 490 BCE, King Darius of Persia launched a seaborne attack on Athens. It was meant as a punishment for its support of a failed rebellion by Greek city-states living under Persian rule on Turkey's west coast. The outnumbered Greek hoplites[5] drove the Persians back into the sea on the beach of Marathon. Ten years later, Xerxes, the new Persian king, seeking to restore Persian honor, organized a vast army and navy designed to conquer all of Greece. Once again, the effort came to grief, principally at the naval battle of Salamis.

One of the sea captains who fought against the Greeks at Salamis was a woman named Artemisia. She was the widowed queen of a city on the southwestern coast of Turkey. In Herodotus' account, King Xerxes watched the battle of Salamis from a hill in the distance. As he watched, Artemisia's ship was being chased by an Athenian. Her path was blocked by a friendly Persian ship. Desperate to escape, she rammed and sank the friendly ship in her way. The Greek ship's captain then assumed that Artemisia was fighting on the Greek side and let her ship go. Watching from a distance, Xerxes assumed that the ship that Artemisia sank was Greek. So Artemisia rose higher in his esteem. "My men," he shouted, "have become women. My women, men!" (Herodotus 8.88–89).

The leader of the men's chorus cites this story to prove that you can't trust women:

Right! For if we give the women here an inch or two,
there's no telling what their slimy hands will try to do.

Maybe build a fleet and launch a treacherous attack.
Persian Artemisia was pretty good at that!

(671–675)

Once the Persians had been defeated, the Athenians joined the Greek city-states on the Aegean Islands and the coast of Turkey in a defensive alliance whose ostensible purpose was defense against Persia. The Athenian fleet provided most of the military force; the other states paid annual dues, tribute in the form of silver coins, for the upkeep of the Athenian fleet.

As time passed there was no evidence of further threats from Persia. The tribute made the Athenians wealthy; their allies resentful. When one or another declared that it was leaving the alliance, the Athenian fleet compelled it to stay. Athens' defensive alliance was becoming an Athenian empire. This worried the other Greeks, none more than their acknowledged leaders, the Spartans.

The Spartans occupied territory in the southeastern Peloponnesus. Their neighbors to the west were the Messenians. In wars of the eighth and seventh centuries BCE, the Spartans conquered and enslaved the Messenians, who were known thereafter as "Helots."[6] With more than enough slaves to grow their food, the Spartans devoted their entire lives to military training. The Spartan hoplite was viewed as Greece's finest soldier.

In 463 BCE, Spartan life was disrupted by an earthquake. The Helots took advantage of the situation to revolt, occupying a stronghold on Mt. Ithome in the northern Messenia. Unable to dislodge the rebels, the Spartans asked the Athenians for help. They complied, sending their best general, Kimon, and 4,000 hoplites. In a short time, something about the Athenians aroused Spartan distrust, and they sent the Athenians home. Feeling insulted, the Athenians withdrew from their alliance with Sparta and joined Sparta's rival Argos instead. The incident marked the beginning of open hostility between Sparta and Athens.

Here, too, Lysistrata changes history radically to suit her political purpose.

Do you recall when Perikleidas came,
the pale-faced Spartan cloaked in red? He sat
in supplication here and begged for help
because Messenia was in revolt
and god was shaking up the Spartan earth?
So Kimon led four thousand hoplites there
and Lacedaemon,[7] thanks to him, was saved!
$$(1138-1144)$$

In 431 BCE, Athens issued a decree forbidding a neighboring town, Megara, from trading with any of Athens' allies. The decree was meant to punish the Megarians for trespassing on sacred Athenian ground. It resulted in severe hardship for them. Alarmed by Athens' imperious action, Sparta and its allies demanded the retraction of the decree. The Athenians refused to take orders from another state. The ultimate result was the Peloponnesian War, which lasted for twenty-seven years. Since Sparta was superior by land and Athens by sea, there were few major battles. The Athenians hunkered down inside their city wall. They let the Spartans to do what damage they could in the Athenian countryside and depended on seaborne raids to wear the Spartans down.

In 425 BCE, the Athenians enjoyed a major victory. The scene of their triumph was Pylos, a small, steep promontory off the southwest coast of the Peloponnesus. There is a bay adjoining the promontory and an island, Sphacteria, lying in the mouth of the bay. The Athenians initiated the encounter by occupying the promontory. The Spartans rushed men and ships to the scene but were unable to capture the promontory, which was too steep. The Spartans tried to establish a beachhead but were driven back. Hence, they settled down to besiege the Athenian stronghold. To surround the Athenians completely, they stationed 420 men on Sphacteria.

That was their fatal mistake. An Athenian fleet operating in the area hurried back to the scene. It routed the Spartan ships that were parked in the bay and encircled the island with their ships, thus trapping the 420 men on Sphacteria.

Eventually the Athenians stormed the island. After a fierce battle, 292 of the 420 Spartans survived and were taken back to Athens as hostages. The Spartans were ready to make peace on terms favorable to Athens. Initially, negotiations were undermined by Cleon, the leader of Athens' war party. When he was killed in battle, advocates for making peace gained power. The result was the Peace of Nicias[8] of 421 BCE.

Aristophanes likened these negotiations to a squabble over a pretty girl, Reconciliation personified:

LYSISTRATA:
It seems we've made a good beginning here.
What's ever gained by war? Why don't you stop?
Why not be reconciled? What's in the way?

SPARTAN DELEGATE:
With one concession we'll comply, to wit:
this mound.

LYSISTRATA:
　Which mound?

SPARTAN ELDER:
The mound called Pylos. Here!
We've loved and fondled it for oh so long!

FIRST ATHENIAN DELEGATE:
No by Poseidon! You're not getting that.

LYSISTRATA:
Oh let it go!

FIRST ATHENIAN DELEGATE:
Then who'll be left to screw?
(1159–1166)

While the Athenians and Spartans had been wearing each other out, Greek city-states on the island of Sicily, led by Syracuse, had been flourishing. As time passed, rivalries broke out among them, and some thought it would be to their advantage to align themselves militarily with the Athenians. In Athens, the prospect of attaching Sicilian states to the Athenian empire was attractive to politicians. Under their influence, the assembly approved dispatching a giant armada to Sicily: 134 triremes, innumerable smaller ships, 5,100 hoplites, an estimated 30,000 combatants in all. The fleet looked invincible, but a bad omen attended its departure.

Miniature statues of Hermes known as Hermae were popular in Athens. Blocks of stone into which faces and genitalia had been carved in appropriate places, they typically stood in the doorways of homes and temples.

One night shortly before the Athenian armada set sail for Sicily, parties unknown mutilated a number of Hermae. Athenians

were extremely upset. Some said that it was part of a plot to establish a tyranny. Others blamed it on inebriated partygoers.

MEN'S LEADER:
I think you'd better buckle up your cloaks.
Some drunken reveler might catch sight of you.

FIRST ATHENIAN DELEGATE:
That sounds like good advice.

SPARTAN ELDER:
  Aye, verily!
  (1093–1096)

The Athenians' famous Sicilian expedition ended in disaster.
The plan had been to starve Syracuse into submission by building a wall enclosing its land side while the Athenian navy blockaded Syracuse's harbor. Syracuse's hoplites, however, prevented
the completion of the wall while their ships' sturdier construction
gave them an advantage over the Athenians' ships, which were
built for speed. After two years of campaigning, the great Athenian armada found itself trapped in the Syracusan harbor. In the
end, the remnants of the Athenian army made a pathetic attempt
to escape by marching overland. Most were overtaken and killed
or enslaved.

The remaining Athenians were terrified at the prospect of
losing control of their empire. Several subject cities did declare
their independence. The wealthiest among them was Miletus on
the Turkish coast, one of Athens' major sources of revenue—and
other items. Aristophanes' characters are able to make light of the
situation. Compare Kalonike's complaint:

It's even hard to find adulterers!
And since Miletus turned to treachery,
I haven't seen a dildo anywhere.
A little leather friend would help a lot!
(107–110)

The Athenians blamed their misfortunes on the foolishness of their reckless young politicians. As a remedy, they appointed ten Commissioners (*Probouloi*) to conduct the war. These were men, all over forty, with reputations for wisdom. The only historical figure known to have served in that capacity was the elderly poet Sophocles. He and the other *Probouloi* served for only one full year, 412 BCE, the dramatic date of *Lysistrata*. It is not known what, if anything, they accomplished in that time. In 411 BCE, they were supplanted by the short-lived oligarchy known as "The Four Hundred." Then the democracy was restored in 410 BCE.

Aristophanes' fictional Commissioner arrives on the scene angry. His appearance fixes the dramatic date of the play at 412 BCE, when the Athenians were in a desperate hurry to rebuild their fleet. The Commissioner had hoped to withdraw money from the Acropolis in order to purchase oars but found its gates locked against him by a mob of women. That, he says, is just another instance of the basic problem with Athens. Its men are too indulgent. For example, women are allowed to engage in ecstatic eastern rites, beating drums, and howling:

Our women's self-indulgence flares again—
the drums, the shouts of "Lord Sabazius,"
Adonis mourned on every household roof.
I heard such cries in our assembly once.
Demostratus, god damn his hide, advised

invading Sicily. His dancing wife
meanwhile was shouting, "O Adonis! Woe!"
He favored adding foreign infantry.
Up on his roof, his evil woman cried,
"Oh flog yourselves for poor Adonis dead."
But he kept on, that filthy, godless twit.
That shows you just how reckless women are.

(387–398)

The idea seems to be that the traditional gods of the state—Zeus, Athena, Apollo—must have been offended by being neglected on such an occasion. Hence the failure of the expedition.

Several passages in *Lysistrata* suggest that eastern rites were popular with the Athenian women at this time and came into criticism from traditionalists; but they were hardly the chief cause of Athens' troubles. The Athenians fought desperately to maintain control of their empire, even winning a major battle. The problem was that the Athenians were using the last of their ships and money. The Spartans, on the other hand, had joined forces with the Persians, and they had unlimited supplies of both.

For Athens, the end came in 405 BCE. Commanded by a ruthless warrior named Lysander, the Spartans destroyed Athens' fleet in the Hellespont and blockaded the city, starving it into submission. The Athenians were compelled to take down their city walls and surrender the foreign territories under their control. They were governed by a group of thirty extreme oligarchs, who oversaw a reign of terror.

In 403 BCE, opponents of the thirty oligarchs who had been organizing in exile marched on the city. After a brief battle, their confrontation issued in a period of negotiations and another restoration of the democracy. The next major event was the trial of Socrates in 399 BCE. Through all this and beyond, Aristophanes kept composing comedies. In his last surviving play, *Wealth* (388 BCE), the blind god of the same recovers his eyesight and starts distributing riches on the basis of merit. This leaves many people unhappy and results in the abandonment of traditional religion. People pray only to *Wealth*. Two later plays were produced by Aristophanes' son.[9] The year of his death is thought to be 386 BCE or thereabouts.

Lysistrata Synopsized

Lysistrata is an example of ancient Greek Old Comedy, a genre of drama that flourished in Athens for the better part of the fifth century BCE. A distinctive feature of Old Comedy is the prominence of a twenty-four-member chorus. As in tragedy, the leader of the chorus engages in conversation with the actors. In the case of *Lysistrata*, there are two semi-choruses of twelve members each. The two groups with their leaders represent the elderly men and women of Athens, respectively. The women support Lysistrata's efforts; the men have to be won over.

All the parts in Old Comedy were actually played by men. A peculiarity of the genre is that the actors and choristers representing men sometimes wore oversized phalluses. The stream of phallus jokes in *Lysistrata* makes it clear that all the actors representing males were equipped with them.

Lysistrata was first performed in the winter of 411 BCE, the twentieth year of the Peloponnesian War. Athens was struggling to recover from a disastrous attempt to conquer Sicily. Behind the scenes, conservatives were plotting to overthrow the democratic constitution. Their efforts would bear fruit in the spring with the dissolution of the democratic assembly and the temporary rule of oligarchs called "The Four Hundred."

With such topical allusions, two choruses abusing each other, giant phalluses, and a subplot that occupies considerable space, the play may seem chaotic, especially to readers sampling Old Comedy for the first time. After working on *Lysistrata* for some time, I have come to think of it as a series of nineteen loosely related comedic skits. The following is my synopsis of the play, together with a selection of direct quotations that illustrate its spirit.

1. A Sacred Oath (1–253)

At the foot of the Acropolis, Lysistrata meets with female representatives of Greece's warring states. Learning that they all hate the war, she reveals her plan for ending it. The women of Greece must swear to withhold sex from their husbands until they make peace.

At first the women are horrified and refuse. Lysistrata finally turns to the gorgeous Lampito, Sparta's representative. She replies in her quaint Spartan dialect:

To sleep without old baldy poking one,
'tis arduous . . . but peace is needed more.
$$(144–145)$$

Lampito's support and Lysistrata's additional urging win over the women.

In addition to the boycott, Athens' female elders will take control of the Acropolis where the state's silver is stored. This will deprive the men of the funds needed to keep the war going.

Lysistrata has all the women swear to abstain from sex until peace is restored. Then shouting is heard on the Acropolis. Lysistrata explains that it is caused by the elderly women taking over the treasury. She and the other Athenian women go to help them. Lampito heads for Sparta to implement Lysistrata's plot there.

2. The Men's Chorus Arrives (254–318)

The Men's Leader is heard leading the male choristers into the orchestra. They have rushed there at the news that women have seized the treasury. Each one carries wood and a smoky fire pot. They plan to burn the women out or to suffocate them.

3. The Arrival of the Women's Chorus (319–349)

The men have caught the attention of the women. They rally to the scene with water jars to put the fire out.

4. An Exchange of Threats Culminates in an Involuntary Bath (350–386)

When the women's chorus falls silent, Men's Leader and Women's Leader notice each other and discover that they are on opposing missions.

MEN'S LEADER:
Hey you, whom all the gods despise, what's with those jars of water?

WOMEN'S LEADER:
So what's the torch for, sepulcher? To set yourself on fire?

MEN'S LEADER:
I'm here to build a pyre, then I'll set your friends on fire!

WOMEN'S LEADER:
I'm here to put that fire out. That's why I've got the water.
(371–374)

Eventually Men's Leader tells a male chorister to set fire to the hair of the Women's Leader. That prompts a counterattack. The women empty their water buckets on the heads of the men.

MEN'S LEADER:
Oimoi! Alas!

WOMEN'S LEADER:
  Too hot for you?

MEN'S LEADER:
  Too hot? I'm freezing, dammit!!

WOMEN'S LEADER:
It's rain to make you bloom again.
(382–383)

5. Enter the Commissioner (387–430)

After the Sicilian disaster, the Athenians granted ten elder states-men the power to propose emergency decrees. In the play, a fictional representative of one of these Commissioners enters the scene angry because he can't withdraw money from the treasury.

To him the event is an example of the bad behavior of women—caused by men spoiling them. According to the Commissioner, the Sicilian invasion was doomed by a politician's wife who sang ill-omened songs while the men debated reinforcements.

6. The Rout of the Scythians (430–466)

The Commissioner has come equipped with crowbars to force his way into the treasury. He is accompanied by slaves and Scythian archers.

The Scythian archers were a peculiar feature of fifth-century Athens. They are believed to have been a force of three hundred state-owned slaves from Scythia. They had the job of keeping order at assemblies and assisting the magistrates in charge of arrests and executions.

The Commissioner is accompanied by four such Scythians. He orders one after another to arrest Lysistrata, but each one is scared away by the threats of an elderly woman. When the Commissioner orders all the archers to charge Lysistrata at once, she reveals that she has an army of warlike women in reserve and orders them to charge. Mostly marketplace women, they stream out through the Acropolis gate, chasing the Scythians away, and return to the Acropolis.

7. The Debate between Lysistrata and the Commissioner (467–613)

The debate has two rounds. Each begins with a choral song and ends in slapstick. In round one, Lysistrata argues that Athens can be saved if the men will listen in silence to women. At the end, she and an elderly woman make the Commissioner put on a woman's veil.

COMMISSIONER:
You pestilence! I'd rather perish than listen in silence
to someone who's wearing a veil.

LYSISTRATA:
Well if *that* is your problem. . . .

(She removes her veil and hands it to him.)

Here is my veil. It covers the head.
Give up your helmet and wear it instead.
If you've something to say, just leave it unsaid.
(530–535)

In round two, Lysistrata argues that the problems that lead to
war can be solved by the patient attention to detail that women
use in untangling balls of wool. She and her elderly friend then
decorate the Commissioner with a garland and ribbons like those
of a corpse being prepared for his funeral.

8. The Choruses Continue the Debate (614–705)

The stage is cleared for performances by the two semi-choruses.
The men complain about the seizure of the treasury. Their concern involves the fact Athenian citizens were paid for serving on
juries, a popular policy among the poor. According to the men's
chorus it was

. . . obvious that Spartan men
convened at Cleisthenes's
and cleverly prevailed upon
the women there to seize

money from the treasury,
the which I can't forgive.
It's funding for the jury-duty
fees I need to live!
                    (616–625)

The women strike a nobler note, listing the honors that they have received in the state's religious rites. They are willing to give life-saving advice in return, but they will not tolerate physical abuse.

If someone hits me now,
his use of teeth is past.
No chewing beans or garlic.
He'll face a total fast.
                    (691–692)

9. Lysistrata Deals with Deserters (706–780)

Lysistrata re-enters the scene, looking worried. Women's Leader asks why. Lysistrata explains that the women camped on the Acropolis have been trying to run away to be with their husbands. As she speaks, four women try to leave with false excuses. One claims to be pregnant, but her swollen belly turns out to be a war helmet hidden under her gown.

Lysistrata wins over the would-be deserters by reading an oracle, which she has just received:

LYSISTRATA:
"When cowering swallows assemble, concealed in a single
    redoubt,
afraid of the well-crested hoopoe, and phallus-wise doing
    without,

there will come a cessation of evil; for Zeus, the great god of
   the sky,
will lower the higher and higher the lower."

TWO WOULD-BE DESERTERS:
We'll lay on the top, you and I!
(770–773)

10. *The Tales of Melanium and Timon (781–828)*

The stage is cleared for another choral performance. The men's
chorus sings about Melanium, a misogynist who lived in the
woods to avoid women. The women's chorus counters with the
misanthrope Timon, who fled human company from his hatred
of evil men. Each story ends with provocative exchanges between
the choruses, for example:

WOMEN'S LEADER:
Should I punch you? Yes or no?

MEN'S LEADER (sarcastically):
I'm so afraid. Please don't, I pray.

WOMEN'S LEADER:
Or I could kick your butt like so.

MEN'S LEADER:
And put your pussy on display?
(821–824)

11. The Sufferings of Kinesias (829–979)

An Athenian male enters. Watching from the Acropolis wall, Lysistrata discovers that he is Myrtle's husband, Kinesias, and tells her how to take advantage of the situation. She is to flirt with him, granting every request except "what the wine cup knows."

Myrtle agrees to lie with Kinesias but thinks of one thing after another that their lovemaking needs: a mattress, perfume, and so on. Then while pretending to undress out of sight, she scampers back through the Acropolis gates, telling Kinesias to remember to vote for peace.

Kinesias is left in a state of pain and confusion.

KINESIAS:
Oh god! These cramps are killing me!

MEN'S LEADER:
And she's the cause of your distress.
She's evil to the nth degree.

KINESIAS:
Yes, she's my sweet, my loveliness!

MEN'S LEADER:
No, you boob! An evil bitch!

KINESIAS:
One or both, I don't know which.
                    (967–972)

12. Is That a Skytalé in Your Loin Cloth? (980–1013)

A herald from Sparta arrives with the news that the Spartans are anxious to make peace. Kinesias has remained on stage. He mocks the Spartan for concealing his sexual predicament:

KINESIAS:
Aha! You've got a giant stiffy there!

SPARTAN HERALD:
Not I, by Zeus! Arrest thy blabbering!

KINESIAS:
Then what is *that*?

SPARTAN HERALD:
A Spartan skytalé.[10]

KINESIAS:
If so, I've got one too. Here, check it out!
(989–992)

Kinesias is glad to hear the Spartan's news. He says that the Athenians are also ready for peace and tells the herald to return to Sparta and ask the authorities to send delegates authorized to make peace.

13. Tears of Joy (1014–1042)

Men's Leader initiates a dialogue with the usual scurrilous criticism of women. This is met with kindness from Women's Leader. She helps Men's Leader put his clothes back on and removes a giant bug from his eye. His tears flow. She steals a kiss. He objects but admits the truth of the saying that one can't live with women or without and declares that henceforth they will be friends forever. The two choruses join hands and begin singing in unison.

14. The Unified Chorus Exhibits an Odd Sense of Humor (1043–1071)

The unified chorus sings a cruelly humorous song. Its theme is the comical plight of poor people for whom a generous promise is suddenly canceled. In the first stanza, the poor are invited to the chorus's house to get all the money they need.

I've got the money. Purses too.
When peace returns and hopes renew,
we shall abolish all the debt
of those who borrowed. Sure, you bet!
$$(1053–1056)$$

The second stanza follows a similar pattern. There the needy are invited to join in a feast given for a wealthy acquaintance. They are even told to bring their children along and walk right up to the mansion—where they will find the door bolted shut.

15. The Gathering of Delegates, Spartan and Athenian (1072–1105)

The Spartan delegates arrive. Their leader engages Men's Leader in conversation. Both sides are suffering. The Athenians fear that they will end up "doing Cleisthenes." The Spartans are afraid that people have seen them masturbating. Both sides are anxious to make peace. Men's Leader suggests summoning Lysistrata. No need. Lysistrata enters on her own.

16. Assisted by Reconciliation, Lysistrata Negotiates Peace (1106–1187)

Lysistrata first summons a goddess, Reconciliation, who appears on the Acropolis wall in the form of a naked girl. Lysistrata then has the delegates stand in rows while she criticizes them. She scolds them for making war on their fellow Greeks when there are well-armed barbarians nearby, and she reminds them of times that they helped each other.

The delegates are more interested in Reconciliation and quickly agree to a lasting peace. Thanks to Lysistrata and Reconciliation, the delegates are all overcome by desire for the peaceful life of farming. Satisfied, Lysistrata invites them all to a feast in the Acropolis. Afterwards, each one may seize his own wife and head for home.

17. Another Musical Interlude (1188–1215)

The unified chorus sings another ode ridiculing the needy. In the first stanza, the chorus asks whether anyone needs fine clothes or jewelry. If so, they should visit the chorus and take anything they find.

Search high and low. Let torches shine.
Take what you find and have a ball.
Unless your eyesight out-sees mine,
you won't find anything at all!
                              (1197–1202)

In the second stanza, it's a family man in need of bread who is invited to the chorus's house. He's invited to bring a sack for Manes, the household slave, to fill. There is just one caveat. Beware of the dog!

18. The Athenian Delegates Leave the Feast (1216–1240)

During the ode, slaves have gathered on stage in front of the Acropolis gate. The drunken, torch-bearing Athenians want to leave the Acropolis, but their progress is blocked by the slaves. The first Athenian thinks about getting a laugh by scorching the slaves with his torch.

Hey fellows! Open up! You're in our way.
What made you choose to sit down there? Perhaps
you want to feel my torch? That old cliché!
I couldn't sink so low! . . . Oh what the hell!
I'll go to any length to please the crowd.

(1216–1220)

He sticks his torch under the gate so that its flame touches one of the slaves. He leaps up and runs away. The chorus laughs.

A second Athenian joins the first and chases another slave away with more laughter. Then the two talk about how much they enjoyed the feast.

19. Musical Finale (1241–1321)

The Spartan delegates come through the gates. One is playing a large panpipe. He asks a companion to hold it for him so that he can perform. "Oh yes!" exclaims the first Athenian delegate, "I love to watch you people sing and dance!" The Spartan obliges with a song celebrating famous victories of the Athenians and Spartans over the Persians.

Lysistrata leads the women out of the Acropolis. Each delegate is joined by his spouse. The first Athenian delegate bursts into a new song. It is a catalog of the gods from whom the Athenian seeks favor. At the end, the Athenian challenges the Spartan to match his latest.

Both the Spartans and the Athenians worshipped Athena. The Athenians did so in the Parthenon on the Acropolis; the Spartans in a more modest but also celebrated temple whose walls were covered with bronze plates. It was known as the bronze house. The Spartan's song exhorts the chorus to sing and dance in Athena's honor.

Now bind your hair and tell your feet
to stomp the meadow floor.
Let your hands clap rhythm while
our choral voices soar
to hymn the goddess housed in bronze,
invincible in war.

(1315–1321)

Biographical Facts

Our knowledge of the literary works of Greek antiquity is based on handwritten Byzantine manuscripts, which are copies of Hellenistic copies of classical originals. A principal source of the texts of Aristophanes' plays is a parchment manuscript from the tenth century CE housed in the public library of Ravenna, Italy.[11] Such manuscripts come equipped with explanatory notes in the margins. Those are known as "scholia." Other information is conveyed in introductory head notes. The latter retail biographical anecdotes about their authors. The manuscripts of Aristophanes contain a relatively long head note with a laudatory account of Aristophanes' career.

According to that, Aristophanes was a native Athenian who lived in the large deme[12] *Kydathenaeon* ("Athenian Glory"), which was located inside the city walls. The Acropolis itself was located inside its boundaries.

The only evidence bearing on the time of Aristophanes' birth are the words of the leader of the chorus in *Clouds* (528–532), speaking as Aristophanes. He says that he considered himself too young at the time of his first play (i.e., 427 BCE) to produce it himself. If he was in his early twenties then, he was born about 450. That would make him about 39 when he wrote *Lysistrata* (i.e., 411 BCE). The last plays attributed to him are datable to 388, implying that he lived at least to 62. Forty-three of his plays are known by title and eleven survive.

Clouds versus Knights

Aristophanes came of age as the war was beginning. Three of his earliest plays (*Babylonians* [lost], *Acharnians*, and *Knights*) dealt critically with the Athenian conduct of the war, especially that of the leader of the war party, the demagogue Cleon. There is no reliable account of how their hostility actually played out. Later generations had Cleon dragging the young playwright into court three times, charged with slander and acquitted each time. As a result, Aristophanes was supposedly hailed as a champion of free speech, and Cleon was forced to pay a fine of five talents.

Aristophanes' *Knights* was relished for its vitriol. His next play, *Clouds*, and those that followed are characterized by a gentler humor. *Clouds* parodies the teaching of the philosopher Socrates. Greek comedies, like tragedies, were performed in competitions at dramatic festivals. *Knights* came in first at the Lenaea, the premier festival for comedies, and *Clouds* came in last. Aristophanes was so upset by this miscarriage that he worked on a revision of the play, which included criticism of the judges for failing to appreciate his finest work.

The Theme of Reconciliation

Aristophanes does seem to have been ahead of his time. Originally, the job of the comic poet was to heap abuse on distinguished citizens. Aristophanes' approach evolved. The actions and mannerisms that he ridicules post-*Knights* are forgivable defects, tragic flaws in reverse. That is clearest in *Lysistrata* where everybody—with the possible exception of the Commissioner—is likable.

Two people stuck in an adversarial relationship sometimes suddenly discover that they are actually very fond of each other. Such is the plot of a number of "romantic comedies." I would suggest that with *Lysistrata*, Aristophanes earned the right to be considered a pioneer in, if not the inventor of, that subgenre. It is not just that Kinesias is reunited with Myrtle after an estrangement, but all it takes for Aristophanes' Spartans and his Athenians to forget a decade of warfare and become best of friends is a friendly feast. Meanwhile the women's leader wins over the men's leader with an act of kindness that reduces him to tears.

When I first studied *Lysistrata*, I found it troubling that the goddess who appears at the end was named *Diallage* ("Reconciliation") instead of *Peace*, but I've come to see things differently. The play focuses on the moments when entrenched hostility disappears and is replaced by affection. Such moments are rare, but they do occur and are precious enough to deserve being personified by a beautiful goddess. To me, that is Lysistrata's universal theme and underlying meaning.

Performance and Translation Notes

My translation is meant to be read aloud or, at least, subvocalized. This poses a problem for nonclassicists, to whom many of the names of persons and places are likely to be unfamiliar. I address that problem by adding footnotes with suggested pronunciations of troublesome terms as they come up in the text. I have tried to include all the names that do not occur in a standard English dictionary. The first appendix, "The Pronunciation of Unfamiliar Names," describes the phonetic symbols that I've used and tries to clarify the rules for locating stresses on polysyllabics.

It is my hope that readers will have fun with this text, reading it expressively, as a Shakespearean actor might do. Virtually the entire text is written in one meter or another, but knowledge of the meters used is not necessary or even helpful. The key is to read with feeling. Nevertheless, for the sake of curious readers I have included a description of the meters in a second appendix, "Meters Used in Translating Spoken Lines." In general, my meters are adaptations of the meters used by Aristophanes with stressed syllables in the English as the functional equivalent of long syllables in the Greek.

In the play, Spartan characters use the Doric dialect, which was actually spoken in Sparta. How to represent this dialectical shift is a hard question for translators. I have kept in mind three facts when considering this question. First, the Spartans were traditionalists. Second, their dialect was used in choral songs. Finally, Aristophanes' version of the Doric dialect is not necessarily accurate. He probably departed from pure Doric to make it more readily intelligible to an Athenian audience and to be amusing. The result might be called mock Doric. With those facts in mind, I have used mock Shakespearean for my Spartan characters. Hopefully, their speeches sound old-fashioned, poetic, and comedic, and are readily intelligible.

As in my previous translations, I have italicized passages that seem on the basis of meter to have been sung. I have translated the spoken passages line by line and numbered them accordingly.

This was impossible in the case of musical passages. For those I just give the line numbers where each one begins and ends.

I did not attempt to weave any fresh scholarly insights into my work on *Lysistrata*. My summary of the historical allusions that occur in the play is based on the venerable *History of Greece to the Death of Alexander the Great* (London: Macmillan, 1900) by J. B. Bury. For the text of the play and enlightening discussions of difficult passages, I relied on Alan H. Sommerstein, *Lysistrata* (Warminster: Aris & Phillips, 1990) and three books by Jeffrey Henderson: *Lysistrata* (Oxford: Clarendon Press, 1987); *Acharnians, Lysistrata, Clouds* (Newburyport, MA: Focus Classical Library, 1988); and *Birds, Lysistrata, Women at the Thesmophoria* (Cambridge, MA: Harvard University Press, 2000).

Notes

1. Constitutions of the city-states varied. Most featured an assembly of all citizens whose powers were limited by a smaller body or council and archons or magistrates with executive powers in specific areas. Athenian democracy was characterized by a particularly powerful assembly.

2. "Tyrant" was not a term of abuse. It was used for any ruler who gained power by force rather than election or inheritance.

3. The biggest event in Athens' religious calendar, a grand procession culminating at the Acropolis with the sacrifice of cattle.

4. Politicians called oligarchs were those who strove to limit the powers of an assembly in favor of the few or, as we might say, the one percent.

5. Hoplites were Greek foot soldiers. They fought in tight formation, wore bronze helmets and breastplates, and carried spears and bronze shields.

6. The etymology of "helot" is unknown. It was applied to persons like the Messenians who had been enslaved en masse in warfare.

7. Lacedaemon, Laconia, and Sparta are used interchangeably to denote the Spartan state. Strictly speaking, Sparta refers to the town; Lacedaemon and Laconia, the region.

8. Nicias was a successful general credited with negotiating the peace treaty of 421. He opposed the later Sicilian expedition but was chosen by the Assembly to lead it. In the end, he was taken prisoner and executed by the Syracusans.

9. The last lost plays are *Cocalus*, after a Sicilian king who murdered Minos while he was looking for Daedalus, and *Aiolosikon*, possibly the name of a character in the play, "Shifty."

10. Skytalés were long thick rods used by Spartans for secret communications. The message was written on leather wrapped around a rod, then unraveled. The recipient read the message by winding the leather around a matching rod.

11. The manuscript was produced by Byzantine scholars working in Constantinople in the tenth century CE. It was presumably brought to Italy when that city fell to the Ottoman Turks in 1453.

12. Athens and its environs were divided for administrative purposes into neighborhoods known as demes.

Lysistrata

Characters

LYSISTRATA (lī-sis´-trə-tä), an Athenian woman

KALONIKE (kä´-lō-nē´-kē), Lysistrata's friendly neighbor

MYRTLE, another Athenian woman; her Greek name, *Myrrhine*, is also the common noun meaning myrtle

Women from Anagyrus (ə-na´-jə-rəs), an Athenian deme

LAMPITO (lam´-pə-tō), a Spartan wife

ISMENIA, a Boeotian wife, mute

CORINTHIAN WIFE, mute

Scythian slave woman

MEN'S CHORUS, twelve elderly male Athenians

MEN'S LEADER, the leader of the male chorus

WOMEN'S CHORUS, twelve elderly female Athenians

WOMEN'S LEADER, the leader of the female chorus

COMMISSIONER, one of the ten Athenian elders elected to guide the Assembly in the wake of the disastrous Sicilian expedition

Commissioner's slaves, two servants carrying crowbars, mute

Scythian archers, four servants of the state, armed archers, mute

OLD WOMEN 1–3, elderly Athenian women who prevent the Scythian archers from apprehending Lysistrata

Lysistrata's army, a large group of women stationed in reserve on the Acropolis, mute except for battle cries

WIVES 1–4

KINESIAS (ki-nē´-sē-əs), a sex-starved Athenian husband

MANES (mä´-nēz), Kinesias's servant, mute; also, slave's name
in a song

CHILD

SPARTAN HERALD

SPARTAN DELEGATES

SPARTAN ELDER

ATHENIAN DELEGATES

RECONCILIATION

(The play is set in ancient Athens at the foot of the Acropolis
during the waning days of the Peloponnesian War between Athens
and Sparta. The action unfolds in front of a gateway. Inside the
gateway there is a stairway leading to the top of the Acropolis where
the Parthenon is found. That holy temple doubles as Athens' treasury. Earlier in the war, it housed thousands of talents of gold and
silver, but in recent days that amount has been spent down con-
siderably in order to build and commission new battleships. Characters enter and exit via aisles on either side of the stage or through
the Acropolis gate. In one passage, there is a conversation between
characters perched on the Acropolis wall and a figure on the
ground below. The choruses enter from the side aisles and occupy
the circular dancing area, the "orchestra" in front of the stage.)

LYSISTRATA:
If you'd announced a feast at Colias,[1]
a shrine of Bacchus, Genetyllis,[2] Pan,

1. Colias (kō´-li-äs), a promontory on the Attic Coast famous for its
temple of Aphrodite.
2. Genetyllis (jə-nə-til´-əs), a minor goddess of childbirth.

you'd see a mob of women beating drums.
As is, there's not a single one!

(Enter KALONIKE.)

   Except
my neighbor, Kalonike!—Well! Hello!

KALONIKE:
Hello, Lysistrata. You seem upset.
You shouldn't frown. You'll hurt your looks that way.

LYSISTRATA:
My blood is boiling over, friend of mine.
I suffer on behalf of womankind.
We hate the way our husbands slander us.   10
We're mischief-makers, so they say.

KALONIKE (aside):
   That's true.

LYSISTRATA:
But call a meeting here to talk about
a serious proposal—sound asleep!
They don't appear!

KALONIKE:
   I think they're coming, dear.
It takes a woman time to get away.
You have to service hubby, don't you know,

then wake the servants, bathe the little kids,
and nurse and rock the baby back to sleep.

LYSISTRATA:
But other things are more important now.   20

KALONIKE:
So tell me what you've got in mind. What is
this thing you've called us all together for?
It must be big!

LYSISTRATA:
   It's huge!

KALONIKE (insinuating):
   And hard as well?

LYSISTRATA:
O yes, by Zee!

KALONIKE:
   Then how come no one's here?

LYSISTRATA:
Because it isn't *that*. That *would* attract
a crowd. It's something else I have in mind.
I've played around with it a lot by night.

KALONIKE:
It must be pretty limp by now, by Zee!

LYSISTRATA:
Yes, if by "pretty limp" you mean the fact
that Greek survival lies in female hands.   30

KALONIKE:
"In female hands"? All's lost! In other words.

LYSISTRATA:
It all depends on us. The way things are,
either the Peloponnesians all must die . . .

KALONIKE:
That's wonderful, by Zee! They won't exist!

LYSISTRATA:
. . . together with Boeotians, all of them.

KALONIKE:
Not all of them. You have to save the eels!

LYSISTRATA:
I dare not speak of Athens's likely fate.
That's up to you to try and figure out.

    (KALONIKE mimes deep thought, then sudden insight
        followed by horror.)

Suppose, however, women gathered here,
Peloponnesians, us, Boeotians too.   40
Coming together *we* could rescue Greece.

KALONIKE:

But how could women manage such a feat?
We'd have to think! That's not our forte. We're good
at looking pretty, wearing saffron gowns,
imported blouses, makeup, fancy shoes.

LYSISTRATA:

The very things in which salvation lies!
Those little dresses, perfumes, fancy shoes,
cosmetic creams, transparent underwear . . .

KALONIKE:

Will rescue Greece? Amazing! How?

LYSISTRATA:

   They'll stop
our few surviving men from hurling spears . . .   50

KALONIKE:

Then by the goddesses,[3] I'll dye my dress!

LYSISTRATA:

. . . or hoisting shields . . .

KALONIKE:

   Where's that imported blouse?

LYSISTRATA:

. . . or wielding swords.

   3. Demeter, goddess of grain, and her daughter Persephone.

KALONIKE:
I'll buy some better shoes.

LYSISTRATA:
So shouldn't they have made it here by now?

KALONIKE:
By now they should have sprouted wings, by Zee!

LYSISTRATA:
They're typical Athenians, you'll see.
They'll spring to action after it's too late.[4]
Nobody's here as yet from Salamis
or from Paralia.[5]

KALONIKE:
   That's no surprise.
They like to ride their steeds[6] at dawn, you know.   60

LYSISTRATA:
Not even those I thought would surely be
among the first to show are present yet,
Acharnians.[7]

---

4. The Athenians reacted to the disastrous Sicilian expedition by econo-
mizing and building a new fleet with surprising rapidity.

5. Paralia (pə-rä´-lē-ä), the name given to the coastal region of Attica.

6. A joke neatly explained by Henderson: "Here [riding steeds] refers to
the coital posture in which the woman bestrides the man" (Lysistrata
[Oxford: Clarendon Press, 1987], 74).

7. Acharnians (ə-kär´-nē-əns), inhabitants of Acharnae, a large, popu-
lous deme in the Attic Plain. Its men were considered extremely warlike.

KALONIKE:

Theogenes's[8] wife
is on her husband's dinghy as we speak.
But look! Here come some other women now.

(Enter MYRTLE and a group of other women.)

LYSISTRATA:

And others over there.

KALONIKE:

Pee-yoo! From where?

LYSISTRATA:

Anagyrus,[9] the land of stinky beans.

KALONIKE:

By Zee! I think somebody "shook the beans."

(LYSISTRATA stares at the newcomers, arms akimbo.)

MYRTLE:

I hope we haven't gotten here too late.
Is something wrong, Lysistrata?

---

8. Several men named Theogenes (thē-ä´-jə-nēz) are ridiculed in Greek comedy. It is not known which one is intended here or why.

9. An Athenian deme was named Anagyrus (ə-na´-ji-rəs) after a wild bean plant, anagyris, that grew there and gave off a bad odor when disturbed. Hence the proverb to which Kalonike alludes; i.e., "Don't shake the anagyris!" = "Let sleeping dogs lie."

LYSISTRATA:
You took   70
your time. We've urgent matters to discuss.

MYRTLE:
I couldn't find my girdle. It was dark.
What are these urgent matters anyway?

LYSISTRATA:
I'll tell you, but we'd better wait awhile
until the Spartan delegates arrive
and those Boeotia sent.

MYRTLE:
That's good advice
'cuz look who's coming now. It's Lampito!

(Enter LAMPITO, ISMENIA, and a CORINTHIAN WIFE.)

LYSISTRATA:
Yes! Welcome dearest Spartan, Lampito!
Your beauty's simply lustrous, sweetie pie!
Your dewy skin! Your powerful physique!   80
Those legs could strangle bulls!

LAMPITO:
I exercise.
I kick my buttocks daily, heels to arse.

MYRTLE (stroking LAMPITO's chest):
You've also got a lovely pair of tits!

LAMPITO:
Desist! I'm not thy sacrificial ox.

LYSISTRATA (indicating ISMENIA):
And where's this other lovely youngster from?

LAMPITO:
Boeotia. She's their chief ambassador,
so help me Twins![10]

MYRTLE:
   She looks the part, by Zee!
Regard her fertile bottom land!

   (Stepping behind ISMENIA, MYRTLE pulls her dress up
      over her head.)

KALONIKE:
   By Zee!
Her herbal garden's neatly trimmed I see.

LYSISTRATA:
And who's this other girl?

LAMPITO:
   A bonny lass   90
from Corinth, s'elp me Twins!

10. Twin gods, Castor and Pollux, Helen's brothers, are frequently invoked by Lampito.

KALONIKE:
It's true, by Zee!

(As she speaks, KALONIKE points to different parts of the
Corinthian's body.)

She's bonny here and there and over here.

(Beat.)

LAMPITO:
Who organized this meeting? Prithee tell!

LYSISTRATA:
That's me.

LAMPITO:
Then ope thy mouth and say outright
what thou wouldst have us do.

KALONIKE:
Oh yes, my dear!
Describe the big, hard thing you have in hand.

LYSISTRATA:
I will, but can I ask a question first?
It's just a little one.

KALONIKE:
Go right ahead!

LYSISTRATA:

Are not your children's fathers sorely missed   100
when they're away campaigning? I'm aware
that all of you have husbands far from home.

MYRTLE:

It's five months now my husband's been in Thrace,
protecting his commander, Eukrates.[11]

KALONIKE:

Mine's been at Pylos[12] seven months at least.

LAMPITO:

Mine cometh home betimes but doth not stay.
He straps his buckler on and flies away.

MYRTLE:

It's even hard to find adulterers!
And since Miletus[13] turned to treachery,
I haven't seen a dildo anywhere.
A little leather friend would help a lot.   110

11. Nothing is known of Eukrates (yü´-krä-tēz) except what can be inferred from the text; i.e., he was an Athenian commander of troops operating in Thrace.

12. Pylos (pī´-lōs), a promontory in Spartan territory on the Peloponnesus' southwest coast. It was seized and fortified by the Athenians in 425 BCE. Its occupation led to the capture of a force of Spartans on an adjacent island. This was Athens' greatest military success to that time in the Peloponnesian War

13. An important tributary ally of Athens and one of several to abandon its alliance with Athens in the wake of the failed Sicilian expedition in 412 BCE.

LYSISTRATA:
Suppose I found a simple way to end
the war, would you be up to helping me?

KALONIKE:
So help me goddesses, I'd pawn my shawl—

(Whispering to ISMENIA.)

Of course, I'd drink the profits right away.

MYRTLE:
I'd be a flounder, slice myself in two,
and donate half of me to end the war.

LAMPITO:
I'd hie me to Taÿgetus's[14] top,
if I could catch a glimpse of peace from there.

LYSISTRATA:
No need to keep it secret any more.
Ladies, there's just one way that we can force   120
our men to make a lasting peace: we must
abstain . . .

KALONIKE:
   Abstain from . . . ?

14. Taÿgetus (tā-i´-jə-təs), a mountain overlooking Sparta, the highest
in the Peloponnesus.

LYSISTRATA:

Promise me you will?

KALONIKE:

Yes! Even in the face of death, I will!

LYSISTRATA:

Okay! We must forgo all contact with . . .

(Beat.)

PENISES.

(The women begin to walk away, muttering and shaking their heads.)

What's going on? You turn your backs to leave?
What's with the angry looks and shaking heads,
the teardrops streaming down your puffy cheeks?
How do you vote? Forgo them, yes or no?

KALONIKE:

Not me! I'd rather let the war creep on.

MYRTLE:

Nor me, by Zee! Let warfare creep along.   130

LYSISTRATA:

But madam flounder! Didn't you declare
you'd slice yourself in two to end the war?

MYRTLE:
Ask something else of me, Lysistrata!
I'd walk through fire happily, I would!
And yet, no more of those? Impossible!

LYSISTRATA (addressing one of the women from Anagyrus):
What about *you*?

WOMAN:
I'll walk through fire, thanks.

LYSISTRATA:
Is our entire gender so depraved?
No wonder tragedies begin with us,
e.g., the tragic tale of Tyro's Tub.[15]

(Addressing LAMPITO.)

Dear Spartan girl, it's down to you alone.   140
If you would vote with me, then maybe we
could save this undertaking.

LAMPITO:
S'elp me, Twins!
To sleep without old baldy poking one,
'tis arduous . . . but peace is needed more.

15. The Greek text refers to "Poseidon and his tub." A scholiast explains that the reference is to the story of the heroine Tyro as dramatized by Sophocles. Tyro was seduced by Poseidon, disguised as a river god, and exposed the twin offspring in a tub in a river. They were saved by a herdsman and grew up to be heroes, the fathers of Nestor and Jason, respectively.

LYSISTRATA:

My dearest dear! The one real woman here!

KALONIKE:

Supposing (gods forbid!) we do abstain
from what you mentioned, will the likelihood
of peace be greater?

LYSISTRATA:

   S'elp me Goddesses,
it will! We'll sit at home with makeup on
in tunics made from fine imported flax,   150
or walk close by, bare naked, muffins plucked.
Our husbands' things will swell. They'll seek relief.
But we'll hang back, resisting stubbornly.
They'll sign a treaty fast. I know they will.

LAMPITO:

They say that Menelaus dropped his sword
when Helen's naked titties caught his eye.[16]

KALONIKE:

What if our husbands spurn us, dear? What then?

LYSISTRATA:

Wear out your canine leather substitute!

16. Euripides invented the detail that, during the fall of Troy, Menelaus spared the unfaithful Helen when he saw her breast; cp. *Andromache* 626–28 (Achilles' father, denouncing Menelaus for causing the Trojan War). "Capturing the woman, you didn't kill her but seeing her breast, you tossed your sword away and stole a kiss."

KALONIKE:
Those imitations! What a waste of time!
What if they drag us toward our rooms and try   160
to ravish us by force?

LYSISTRATA:
  Then grab the door.

KALONIKE:
What if they beat us?

LYSISTRATA:
  Yield ungraciously.
They don't enjoy the act when using force.
So be a total bitch. Don't worry, girl.
They'll soon give up. A man cannot enjoy
his life unless he has a happy wife.

KALONIKE (sighing after long silence):
If both of you agree, then so do we.

LAMPITO:
We can convince *our* men to keep the peace.
They won't resort to underhanded tricks;
but what about thy scurvy riffraff, eh?   170
Can anything restrain those lunatics?

LYSISTRATA:
Relax, my friend. They're under our control.

LAMPITO:

Thy triremes[17] have their rigging still. What's worse,
thy goddess hath no end of silver coin.[18]

LYSISTRATA:

We've taken care of all contingencies.
Th' Acropolis will fall to us today.
While older women seize the treasury
by faking sacrificial rites up there,
we'll be arranging matters here below.

LAMPITO:

I cannot fault thy plan or lucid speech.   180

LYSISTRATA:

Then let's make things official with an oath,
an iron-clad commitment, right away.

LAMPITO:

Wilt thou describe the aforementioned oath?

---

17. Triremes were Greek warships featuring three banks of oars and
bronze beaks for ramming enemies. Athens' fleet of triremes was the foun-
dation of its military power.

18. The most common coin among the ancient Greeks was the silver
drachma, which was the daily wage of a rower in the fleet. Wealth was mea-
sured in "talents," which stood for 6,000 drachmas each. At the beginning of
the war, the Athenians established an emergency fund of 1,000 talents or
6,000,000 drachmas. Cp. Bury, *History of Greece to the Death of Alexander the
Great* (London: Macmillan, 1900), 488.

LYSISTRATA:
Okay! But where's the Scythian![19] Wake up!

(Scythian attendant hurries out of the gates carrying a
    shield.)

Now place that shield before me upside down.
Somebody bring the victims now!

KALONIKE:
  What kind
of vow is this, Lysistrata?

LYSISTRATA:
  What kind?
It's Aeschylean.[20] He collected blood
of sheep in shields like this.

KALONIKE:
  Whoever's heard
of making vows concerning peace on shields!   190

19. In the mid-fifth century, the Athenians purchased three hundred
slaves to help preserve public order and assist magistrates. These slaves were
called Scythian archers, although it is not clear that they were actually eth-
nic Scythians or archers.

20. Lysistrata's ceremony parodies a passage in Aeschylus' tragedy *Seven
Against Thebes* 42–48. There heroic warriors fill an overturned shield with
bull's blood. Each swears to fight to the death while touching the blood.
Lysistrata fills a wide-mouthed jar with wine and has all her companions
touch it while swearing to withhold sex from their husbands.

LYSISTRATA:
And what about the victim?

KALONIKE:
   Let's obtain
a horse somewhere, a stallion, shiny white.

LYSISTRATA:
Who's got a horse?

KALONIKE:
   What's your suggestion then?

LYSISTRATA:
I'll tell you if you really want to know.
We'll put a giant loving cup down here,
decanting jars of wine in it, and vow
we'll never let a drop of water in.

LAMPITO:
Huzzah! The very paragon of oaths!

LYSISTRATA:
Somebody, quick! Go get a jar and cup.

   (The Scythian hurries down a side passage out of sight. Beat.
     The Scythian returns carrying an amphora full of wine and
     a very large drinking cup.)

MYRTLE:
My goodness, ladies! What terrific jugs!   200

   (The Scythian places the drinking cup in front of
     LYSISTRATA and gives her the amphora.)

KALONIKE:
To touch this jar is sudden ecstasy!

LYSISTRATA:
Hands off! Now everybody stroke this . . . pig.

   (All place their hands on the rim of the drinking cup.)

Lord Loving Cup and Mistress Eloquence,
kindly accept this female sacrifice.

   (She pours wine into the cup.)

MYRTLE:
Its blood is nice and red and gushes well.

LAMPITO:
By Castor, yes! A brave aroma too!

MYRTLE:
With your permission, ladies, I'll go first.

KALONIKE:
By Cypris, not unless you draw the lot!

LYSISTRATA:
Stop! All of us including Lampito
must touch the cup while one of us   210
recites this oath on everyone's behalf:

   (One after another, each woman solemnly places her hand on
        the rim of the cup. LYSISTRATA begins the oath, nodding
        at KALONIKE.)

Let no one, husband or adulterer . . .

KALONIKE:
Let no one, husband or adulterer . . .

LYSISTRATA:
Come near me with a throbbing stiffy.

   (Beat.)

   Speak!

KALONIKE:
Come near me with a throbbing stiffy. . . . Speak!
My knees are giving way, Lysistrata!

LYSISTRATA:
I'll stay at home and lead a virgin's life . . .

KALONIKE:
I'll stay at home and lead a virgin's life . . .

LYSISTRATA:
wearing a saffron gown and facial paint . . .

KALONIKE:
wearing a saffron gown and facial paint . . .   220

LYSISTRATA:
to drive my husband mad with lust for me.

KALONIKE:
to drive my husband mad with lust for me.

LYSISTRATA:
But I will never willingly submit . . .

KALONIKE:
But I will never willingly submit . . .

LYSISTRATA:
and if he uses force against my will . . .

KALONIKE:
and if he uses force against my will . . .

LYSISTRATA:
I'll lie completely still and make a face.

KALONIKE:
I'll lie completely still and make a face.

LYSISTRATA:
No raising Persian slippers toward the roof!

KALONIKE:
No raising Persian slippers toward the roof!   230

LYSISTRATA:
No crouching down on all fours like the lioness on my bronze
    cheese grater!

KALONIKE:
No crouching down on all fours like the lioness on Lysistrata's
    bronze cheese grater!

LYSISTRATA:
To solemnize these vows, I'll drink from here.

KALONIKE:
To solemnize these vows, I'll drink from here.

LYSISTRATA:
Should I transgress, let water fill my cup!

KALONIKE:
Should I transgress, let water fill my cup!

LYSISTRATA:
Do all of you swear too?

ALL:
    By Zee, we do!

LYSISTRATA:
I'll pour the first libation.

(She takes a drink.)

KALONIKE:
  Careful, dear!
Don't drink too much. Let's keep it friendly here.

(Shouts and cries are heard.)

LAMPITO:
Whence came that hubbub?

LYSISTRATA:
  Just what I explained.   240
We've seized the goddess's Acropolis.
The women have it now. So Lampito,
set forth to Sparta. Make arrangements there,
leaving these ladies here as hostages,
while we ourselves assist the older ones,
who need to bar the gates. We'll hurry there.

KALONIKE:
But don't you fear the men will rally soon
and try to overpower us?

LYSISTRATA:
  Who cares?
They don't have threats or fire strong enough
to make us open up these temple gates   250
without accepting terms that we propose.

KALONIKE:
You're right, by Aphrodite! Otherwise,
don't call us total bitches anymore!

> (All exit, LAMPITO via a side passage; the others through
> the Acropolis gates. The MEN'S LEADER enters via a side
> passage, followed by MEN'S CHORUS. All carry logs and
> fire pots.)

MEN'S LEADER:
Keep marching, Drakes! Lead the way!
    Ignore your aching shoulder.
Don't let that load of olive trunks
    defeat your manly spirit.

> (The MEN'S CHORUS files into the orchestra. They chant,
> then break into song.)

MEN'S CHORUS:

How many things you don't foresee   Strophe 1 (256–270)
   occur as you get older!
Who would have thought the women we   260
   begot and raised so kindly

would seize Athena's statue
   and my Acropolis
and seal the sacred precinct with
   bolts and bars like this!

MEN'S LEADER:
Let's hurry to the citadel!
    Come on the run, Philurgus!

We're off to trap the women there,
  surrounding them with kindling.
We'll get the sluts who planned the crime
  and then we'll get their helpers.
Then build a pyre nice and high,
  and when it smokes and hisses
we'll take a vote, then kill them all
  —and start with Lykon's missus.[21]   270

MEN'S CHORUS:
We guarantee these women won't   Antistrophe 1 (271–285)
  be laughing any longer!
Cleomenes,[22] a king no less,
  once occupied the Polis.[23]
He didn't leave triumphant though
  he claimed to be a Spartan!

He gave up shield and weapons
  walking down surrender's path

21. Lykon (lī´-kän), a prominent Athenian whose wife had a bad reputation. The comic poet Eupolis (fragment 232) is quoted as saying that "every man found a way to her."

22. Cleomenes (klē-ä´-mə-nēz), a Spartan king who twice intervened militarily in Athenian politics. In 510 BCE, he forced the tyrant Hippias and the other Peisistratids to abandon Athens by taking their children hostage. Two years later, he and his Athenian allies seized the Acropolis in the hope of replacing Cleisthenes' democratic reforms with an oligarchic constitution. A popular uprising by the Athenian people forced him to abandon the occupation after only two days. This was a pivotal event in the history of western democracies. Cp. Herodotus 5.62–66 and 72.

23. Polis is a common noun meaning city or city-state. The Men's Chorus uses it here and elsewhere as shorthand for the Acropolis.

and looked a mess, as though he'd gone
    six years without a bath.   280

MEN'S LEADER:
The treatment that he got from me was
    positively savage!
I blocked the gates with seventeen
    platoons of hoplite soldiers.
How could you think I'd find it hard
    to teach these women manners,
these enemies of gods and men,
    also Euripides's?
My monument at Marathon
    go on and smash to pieces!

MEN'S CHORUS:
The ascent to the Polis is all that remains   Strophe 2 (286–295)
of this trip. How I wish I was already there!

But I cannot imagine our reaching the top
with no mules to help carry the load that we bear.   290

These logs, for example, they're breaking my back,
but I have to keep going although it is broke

and blow on these cinders. They mustn't go out!
Wah-choo! Had to sneeze! How I hate all this smoke!

Some monster attacks me. O lord
    Heracles!   Antistrophe 2 (296–305)
It began its invasion by biting my eyes,

when it leapt from my jar like a ravenous bitch,
or a Lemnian fire[24] with all that implies,   300

for that would explain its ferocious attack.
Let's get to the Polis! This isn't a joke.

It's now or it's never. The goddess needs help.
Wah-choo! Had to sneeze! How I hate all this smoke!

MEN'S LEADER (blowing in his fire pot):
Come see! My flame is waking up.
    Why thank you, gods! It's burning!
So what's to do? Suppose we drop
    our lumber here for starters,
then use these vines as fire brands
    and set them all to blazing.
When they ignite, we'll make like rams
    and madly charge the portals!
We'll shout, "Unlock the gates!"
    And what if they refuse to?   310
Why then we'll burn the gateway down
    and suffocate the women.
So drop your logs. Wah-choo! This smoke!
    It's only getting thicker.
A little help from Samos,[25] please!
    so we can do it quicker.

24. The island of Lemnos was the site of active volcanoes and the supposed location of Hephaestus' forge. In mythology, the women of Lemnos murdered all the island's men for fooling around with Thracian women. As a result, "Lemnian" came to connote extreme wickedness.

25. At the time of *Lysistrata*'s performance the Athenian fleet was stationed at the Aegean Island of Samos struggling to hold the Athenian empire together.

> (He sets his jar and twigs down on the ground, unstraps the
> logs on his back, and sets them down too. His actions are
> imitated by the other choristers.)

Ah! What relief! My spine is not
    being tortured any longer!

> (He holds torch over his jar with its flickering flame—with
> little effect.)

Now pot, you've got a duty too:
    to set this fuel on fire.
Come on! Let's go! Or can't you make
    the torch's flame go higher?
Queen Victory, we'd love to raise
    above those horrid women
who dared to seize our Polis, one
    enormous battle trophy.

> (The male choristers huddle over their fire pots on one side
> of the orchestra while the WOMEN'S LEADER and the
> WOMEN'S CHORUS enter from a lateral passage into the
> other side.)

WOMEN'S LEADER:
I see a cloud of smoke and sparks.
    It's rising ever higher.
We'd better get there quickly, girls.
    The situation's dire.   320

WOMEN'S CHORUS:

Now spread your wings and fly to us,　　　　　　　　　Strophe 3 (321–335)
　　sweet Nikodika do,
for Calyx otherwise will burn
　　and poor Crytilla too.

They're buffeted by nasty winds
　　and geezers full of hate.
I'm terribly afraid that we
　　will get to them too late.

I filled my water jar just now.
　　Did so at break of day.
The noisy crowd and clatter such
　　I barely got away.

Maids and branded slaves were there.
　　They poked and prodded me.
In point of fact, I didn't care.　　　　　　　　　　　　　　330
　　I worked efficiently.

I've come to save my neighbors now,
　　and help prevent a slaughter
for they'll be set on fire (Ow!)
　　if we don't bring them water.

I've heard some foolish older men　　　　　　　　Antistrophe (336–349)
　　approach the citadel
with loads of kindling that would serve
　　a bath's attendant well.

They're shouting terrifying threats.
    They call us ugly names.
They say they must consign the vile
    women here to flames.   340

I wouldn't choose to see them burn,
    o goddess we adore.
I'd rather watch them saving Greece
    from lunacy and war.

That's the only reason why
    they seized your sacred towers.
They call you golden champion.
    I pray that you'll be ours.

O goddess born by Triton's lake,[26]
    O Zeus's favorite daughter,
if any man sets them aflame,
    help us bring them water.

    (WOMEN'S LEADER and MEN'S LEADER notice each
    other.)

WOMEN'S LEADER:
Be quiet, please! What's this one sees? A flock of good-for-
    nothings.   350
They don't resemble gentlemen to judge by what they're doing.

---

26. Athena's enigmatic epithet, *Tritogeneia* (Triton-born) gave rise to
the story that she was born or raised by a legendary body of water known as
Triton's Lake.

MEN'S LEADER:

What meets our eyes? An unforeseen development is
    brewing,
a female swarm is here to help their friends attack the Polis.

(The MEN'S LEADER farts.)

WOMEN'S LEADER:

You're flatulent from fear, my dear. Perhaps our numbers
    frighten?
Well if they do, I'm telling you: we're just a tiny fraction.

MEN'S LEADER:

O Phaedrias, how much of this foul noise should we put up
    with?
Let's break some sticks across their backs. Somebody needs
    to spank them.

WOMEN'S LEADER:

Okay, let's set our pitchers down in case somebody charges.
We wouldn't want to let our jars restrict our counterpunches.

MEN'S LEADER:

If Hipponax[27] was only here! He'd stop your ugly chatter.   360
His old one-two would silence you. Ask Bupalus the
    sculptor.

27. Hipponax was a mid-sixth-century BCE poet of Ephesus famous for
abusive verse. His favorite target was a sculptor, Bupalus, who once exhib-
ited an unflattering bust of Hipponax. Supposedly, the poet then denounced
the sculptor so viciously in verse that he hanged himself!

WOMEN'S LEADER:

Well check it out. I'm standing here. Somebody, come and try
    me!

No angry bitch has sharper teeth. Prepare to lose your testes.

MEN'S LEADER:

Shut up unless you want my fists to wreck your ancient body!

WOMEN'S LEADER (indicating the biggest female chorister):

Why don't you try Stratyllis here? Just poke her with your finger.

MEN'S LEADER:

Suppose I bash your face instead. I'll use my manly knuckles.

WOMEN'S LEADER:

Why, you'd be ripped apart. I'd eat your lungs and your
    intestines!

MEN'S LEADER:

No animals that live on earth are wickeder than women.

Euripides will tell you that, and no one's any wiser.

WOMEN'S LEADER:

Attention, girls! Pick up your jars! Snap to it there,
    Rhodippe!   370

MEN'S LEADER:

Hey you, whom all the gods despise, what's with those jars of
    water?

WOMEN'S LEADER:
So what's the torch for, sepulcher? To set yourself on fire?

MEN'S LEADER:
I'm here to build a pyre, then I'll set your friends on fire!

WOMEN'S LEADER:
I'm here to put that fire out. That's why I've got the water.

MEN'S LEADER:
You think you'll put my fire out?

WOMEN'S LEADER:
    You'll see it done in person.

MEN'S LEADER:
Suppose I take this torch of mine and set your feet on fire?

WOMEN'S LEADER:
Then if you've got a bar of soap, I'll bathe you very nicely.

MEN'S LEADER:
A bath from you, you garbage heap?

WOMEN'S LEADER:
    Just like your wedding morning.

MEN'S LEADER:
I don't believe your insolence!

WOMEN'S LEADER:
   We citizens speak freely.

MEN'S LEADER:
I'll see you silenced some day soon.

WOMEN'S LEADER:
   You're not on jury duty.   380

MEN'S LEADER (threatening her with his torch):
Somebody, set her hair aflame!

WOMEN'S LEADER:
   It's time to help me, river!

   (WOMEN'S LEADER pours water on MEN'S LEADER.
      The female choristers do the same on their male
      counterparts.)

MEN'S LEADER:
Oimoi! Alas!

WOMEN'S LEADER:
   Too hot for you?

MEN'S LEADER:
   Too hot? I'm freezing, dammit!!

WOMEN'S LEADER:
   It's rain to make you bloom again.

MEN'S LEADER:
Oh yeah? I'm dry from trembling.

WOMEN'S LEADER:
You've got your fire pot right there. Use that for self-defrosting.

(Enter the COMMISSIONER accompanied by two slaves and
four Scythian archers. The COMMISSIONER and the
slaves carry crowbars. Meanwhile the male choristers
angrily take off their wet clothing to shake off the water.)

COMMISSIONER:
Our women's self-indulgence flares again—
the drums, the shouts of "Lord Sabazius,"[28]
Adonis[29] mourned on every household roof.
I heard such cries in our assembly once.   390
Demostratus,[30] god damn his hide, advised
invading Sicily. His dancing wife
meanwhile was shouting, "O Adonis! Woe!"
He favored adding foreign infantry.
Up on his roof, his evil woman cried,

28. Sabazius (sä-bä´-zē-əs), a Phrygian god often identified with Dionysus.
29. Adonis was a youth loved by Aphrodite and killed by a boar while
hunting. In summer, women planted short-lived flowers on rooftops and
lamented his death over the wilted blooms.
30. Demostratus (də-mäs´-trä-təs), it is not known which occasion the
speech referenced here was given. It was evidently not when the expedition
was first authorized, since that occurred in spring, whereas the ill-omened
Adonis ritual, supposedly happening in the background, was held in mid-
summer. See Sommerstein, *Lysistrata* (Warminster: Aris & Phillips, 1990),
173, for a detailed discussion.

"Oh flog yourselves for poor Adonis dead."
But he kept on, that filthy, godless twit.
That shows you just how reckless women are!

MEN'S LEADER (indicating the WOMEN'S CHORUS):
And what about *these* female criminals?
Among their violent crimes, they gave us baths!   400
From jars! That's why we're shaking out our clothes,
and everybody thinks we peed on them!

COMMISSIONER:
By salty lord Poseidon, serves us right!
For we're accomplices ourselves and teach
our women how to gratify their lust.
So naturally their wicked schemes abound.
Just think of how we talk in public shops.
"Goldsmith! You know the necklace you repaired?
Last night my wife—she's dancing. All at once,
she sees the prong has left its aperture.   410
This evening I'll be bound for Salamis.
So if you're free, be sure and visit then.
Enlarge the prong. Make sure it fills the hole."
Another chats a leather worker up,
a youngster, but his prong is fully grown.
"My woman's little toe is suffering
Her sandal strap is choking it to death,
poor tender thing! Why don't you visit her
at noon some day and help her loosen it."
Such conversations lead to evil acts.   420
Though your commissioner, that's me, found wood

for oars and needs the funds to purchase some,
the women here have locked the Polis gates!

(Addressing his slaves.)

No use just standing there. Use crowbars now!
Let's pry these women loose from arrogance!

(The COMMISSIONER's slaves stare at him with puzzled
expressions.)

What are you slack-jawed morons staring at?
Did I say "Rest!" or "Find a winery!"
No! Stick your crowbars underneath the gates
and pry them up from there. I'll do the same
from over here.

(Enter LYSISTRATA through the gates.)

LYSISTRATA:
Don't pry from anywhere.   430
I'm coming on my own. What need is there
of crowbars? What you need is common sense.

COMMISSIONER:
Oh really, scabies? Where'd the archers go?

(Addressing ARCHER 1, who steps forward.)

Grab her and bind her hands behind her back!

LYSISTRATA:
If he just lays a fingertip on me,
by Artemis, he'll be one sorry slave!

   (ARCHER 1 makes menacing gestures but doesn't actually
       attack LYSISTRATA.)

COMMISSIONER:
Afraid?

   (Addressing ARCHER 2, who also responds with futile
       gestures.)

   He needs assistance. Grab her waist,
then bind her, both of you, and hurry up!

OLD WOMAN 1 (entering through the gate):
By Pandrosus![31] Just lay a hand on her,
I'll batter you until you shit your shorts!   440

COMMISSIONER:
Until I what? Another archer please!
First bind *her* hands, the blabbermouth, I mean.

   (ARCHER 3 steps forward, gesturing. Enter OLD
       WOMAN 2.)

---

31. Pandrosus (pan´-drə-səs), a daughter of Kekrops, the mythical first
king of Athens.

OLD WOMAN 2:
If you just lay a fingertip on her,
By Phosphorus,[32] I'll blacken both your eyes.

COMMISSIONER:
What's this and where's an archer?

(To ARCHER 4.)

Capture *her.*
We'll overpower one of them at least.

(Enter OLD WOMAN 3.)

OLD WOMAN 3:
Go on! Try touching her, by Artemis!
I'll tear your hair out by its bloody roots.

COMMISSIONER:
Oh no! I'm out of archers! Dammit all!
Men can't admit defeat at female hands.   450
Not ever! Battle stations, Scythians!
Now charge!

(The Scythians have formed a line but are too cowardly to
    charge.)

32. Phosphorus (fäs´-fər-əs), "Light-bringer," a title of Hecate, a goddess
associated with the dark arts and popular with Athenian women.

LYSISTRATA:
　　Now by the goddesses, it's time
you learned that we've assembled four platoons
of warlike women, fully armed, within.

COMMISSIONER:
You Scythians! Advance and twist their arms!

LYSISTRATA:
You women warriors within, come out!
Come stew-and-cabbage-selling market girls!
Inn-keeping, bread-and-garlic-serving girls!
Come on and scratch them, hit them, beat them up!
Abuse them! Use your worst obscenities!　　　　　　　460

　　(LYSISTRATA's army emerges from the Acropolis gate. As
　　　LYSISTRATA urges them on, the women charge, routing
　　　the archers while shouting vulgar taunts. The rout
　　　continues until the archers are driven away.)

Enough. Come back. No need to get their arms.

　　(The archers flee via a side passageway. OLD WOMAN 1
　　　lingers around the gate; OLD WOMEN 2 and 3 and
　　　LYSISTRATA's army return from the chase and exit via the
　　　Acropolis gate.)

COMMISSIONER:
Those Scythians! They really let me down!

LYSISTRATA:

You shouldn't be surprised. Perhaps you thought
we'd fight like slaves or else you hadn't heard
about a woman's wrath.

COMMISSIONER:

   I heard it's great
when they're around an open winery.

MEN'S LEADER:

Look, national commissioner, you've gotten pretty wordy.
But what's the point of lengthy talk with beasts like these
   subhumans?
Or don't you know about their crime, their soaking us with
   water?
And we were not prepared, i.e. being fully dressed and
   soapless!   470

WOMEN'S LEADER:

You shouldn't fight with neighbors, friend, without sufficient
   reason.
For when you do, it's often true, you end up bruised and swollen.
I would prefer to sit at home, a quiet little maiden,
not causing pain to anyone, not starting any trouble;
but poke my nest, you'll raise a wasp, and not without a stinger.

MEN'S CHORUS:

Zeus, tell us what we ought to do   Strophe (476–483), cp. 541–548
   with these monstrosities.
I say we try to ascertain
   whatever made them seize   480

the fortress where Cranaus[33] ruled,
 the rocky precipice,
the sacred precinct overhead,
 our great Acropolis.

MEN'S LEADER:
Examine her strictly! Dispute every word that she utters!
We cannot approve such an act without knowing its motive.

COMMISSIONER:
Agreed! And I'm eager to ask her the following question:
Could you kindly explain why you've blocked the Acropolis
 entrance?

LYSISTRATA:
To be certain our silver is safe and not wasted on warfare.

COMMISSIONER:
So silver's the cause of our wars?

LYSISTRATA:
 And of all of our troubles!
Take Pisander[34] and other officials. They're constantly
 causing   490

---

33. Cranaus (crä-nā´-əs), the second king of Athens in its mythical history.

34. Pisander (pi-san´-dər), an influential politician. At the time that *Lysistrata* was produced, he was secretly promoting plans for an oligarchic coup aimed at forming an alliance with the Persians. His activities are fully recounted in Thucydides' eighth book; see paragraphs 49, 53, 54, 56, 63, 67, 68, 90, and 98.

more trouble in order to steal. Let them do what they
    want to,
so long as they're no longer spending our silver to do it.

COMMISSIONER:
But what would *you* do with it?

LYSISTRATA:
    Do? Why, we'll be its comptrollers.

COMMISSIONER:
You mean *you* will take charge of our silver!

LYSISTRATA:
    You find that surprising?
Or haven't you noticed we handle domestic expenses?

COMMISSIONER:
That's different!

LYSISTRATA:
    Oh really?

COMMISSIONER:
    We have to fight wars with that silver.

LYSISTRATA:
That's not a necessity.

COMMISSIONER:
    No? It's our only salvation!

LYSISTRATA:
We'll be your salvation!

COMMISSIONER:
  You women?

LYSISTRATA:
  You heard me.

COMMISSIONER:
  You're joking!

LYSISTRATA:
You'll survive if you want to or not.

COMMISSIONER:
  That's absurd!

LYSISTRATA:
  You're indignant.
No matter. We'll do what we must.

COMMISSIONER:
  But your action's illegal!   500

LYSISTRATA:
You have to be saved!

COMMISSIONER:
  Even though we're not asking?

LYSISTRATA:
The more so.

COMMISSIONER:
You constantly talk about war. What accounts for your interest?

LYSISTRATA:
I'm happy to tell you.

COMMISSIONER:
Make it quick or prepare for a beating.

LYSISTRATA:
Just listen and practice controlling your fists if you're able.

COMMISSIONER:
When I'm angry, they're hard to control.

OLD WOMAN 1:
If you don't, you'll regret it!

COMMISSIONER:
Go croak to yourself! Let Lysistrata talk to me.

OLD WOMAN 1:
Gladly!

LYSISTRATA:
In the past, from our sense of "the proper," we women supported whatever you husbands proposed. We listened in silence.

As a matter of fact, you prohibited voicing objections.
But even at home we could follow the gist of your
    speeches   510
and often we'd hear you adopting disastrous proposals.
Then concealing our pain with a smile we would ask you a
    question,
like "What was decreed in assembly concerning the treaty?
Did you vote to amend it?" "So what if we did?" you would
    thunder
and tell me I'd better be silent. And so I was silent.

OLD WOMAN 1:
Me—I had spoken!

COMMISSIONER:
    And soon you'd be weeping.

LYSISTRATA:
    That's why I was silent.
But then I would learn of some even more foolish decision,
and ask a new question like "Husband, what's driving you
    crazy?"
At that he would angrily tell me to tend to my weaving
or he'd batter my head because "war is the business of
    men."[35]   520

COMMISSIONER:
Say what you like but old Homer was right about that!

    35. A famous quotation from Homer's *Iliad* (6.492). Hector delivers this
opinion while dismissing his wife's sensible recommendations.

LYSISTRATA:
He was right that we never should question a foolish decision?
Still it wasn't until you began lamentation in public,
afraid that the army had perished without a survivor,
that we finally decided to act for the safety of Hellas,
we women together. No reason to wait any longer.
If you're willing to listen to helpful suggestions in silence,
like we used to do, we'll be only too happy to save you.

COMMISSIONER:
You! Save us! What you say is outrageous.

LYSISTRATA:
   I said to be quiet!

COMMISSIONER:
You pestilence! I'd rather perish than listen in silence   530
to someone who's wearing a veil.

LYSISTRATA:
   Well if *that* is your problem . . .

(She removes her veil and hands it to him.)

Here is my veil. It covers the head.
Give up your helmet and wear it instead.
If you've something to say, just leave it unsaid.

OLD WOMAN 1 (handing him a basket containing wool):
This wool is for carding and now it's your turn.
To be a wool worker is easy to learn,
and war from now on is the woman's concern.

WOMEN'S LEADER (addressing the WOMEN'S CHORUS):
It's time to rise and dance once more; so, ladies, leave your
  pitchers
and give your full support again to your beloved sisters.   540

WOMEN'S CHORUS:
I will! No dance will wear me out,

> Antistrophe (541–548), cp. 476–483

  no kicking sprain my knees.
I'll face most anything at all
  with women such as these.
For they're endowed with excellence,
  with courage, grace, and heart.
They're wise and patriotic too,
  virtuous and smart.

WOMEN'S LEADER:
Most valiant of grandmas and matrons with prickly
  vaginas,
attack with a passion! Don't soften! The wind's at your
  back!   550

LYSISTRATA:
If only sweet Eros and Cyprian-born Aphrodite
will help us by filling our bosoms and thighs with desire,
our men with enjoyable stiffness and swollen extensions,
some day we'll be hailed as the battle-disbanders of Greece.

COMMISSIONER:
For accomplishing what?

LYSISTRATA:

The prevention of men wearing armor
from crowding the market like Maenads.

OLD WOMAN 1:

O yes Aphrodite!

LYSISTRATA:

They wander around to examine ceramics and cabbage,
all over the agora, heavily armed Corybantes.[36]

COMMISSIONER:

They're men, so they have to be manly!

LYSISTRATA:

I call them pathetic.
One carries a gorgon-head shield when he shops for
anchovies!   560

OLD WOMAN 1:

I witnessed a pony-tailed cavalry officer filling
his helmet with porridge he stole from an elderly woman,
and a Thracian who brandished his arms like he thought he
    was Tereus.[37]
He panicked the fig girl and ate all the figs in her basket!

36. Corybantes (kȯ-rə-ban´-tēz), wildly emotional priests of the eastern
mother goddess, Cybele.

37. Tereus (tē´-rüs), a mythical Thracian king married to an Athenian
princess. He raped her sister and cut off her tongue to prevent her from talking. For the whole story see Ovid, *Metamorphoses* 6.424–674.

COMMISSIONER:
So how would you women be able to solve the profusion
of problems perplexing us?

LYSISTRATA:
Ever so simply.

COMMISSIONER:
So tell us!

LYSISTRATA:
It's the way that we handle a tangle of yarn when we're spinning.
We separate threads from each other wherever one dangles.
That's how we'll untangle this war if you gentlemen let us—
by loosening threads from each other wherever they
dangle.   570

COMMISSIONER:
If you think that your baskets of wool and your spindles and
bobbins
can settle our conflicts, you're fools!

LYSISTRATA:
If your head weren't so empty,
our spindles and bobbins would teach you political science.

COMMISSIONER:
Oh really?

LYSISTRATA:
The city's a fleece; so your first obligation
is washing the sheep shit away in a basin of water.

Then give it a beating. Get rid of the riffraff and rabble.
And what about citizens squeezing themselves into factions
and running for office? They call for a comb and a scissors.
It's off with their heads! But the migrants and foreign
    connections?
All of them go in a basket of mutual kindness.   580
Even a person in debt to the state's in that basket,
plus all the colonial cities that Athens has founded.
The latter are clusters of yarn that are yours for the asking.
They're scattered, however. So gather this yarn from those
    cities,
then splice it together in Athens and use it for making
a mountainous bobbin and weaving the city a mantle.[38]

COMMISSIONER:
You've plenty of nerve to be speaking of spindles and bobbins,
considering you have no part in the war.

LYSISTRATA:
    Are you kidding?
The worst of its hardships are ours. There's the bearing of
    children,
the sons that we raise to be soldiers.

COMMISSIONER:
    Don't mention past sorrows!   590

38. Lysistrata's proposal boils down to the elimination of undesirables from Athenian citizenship and the inclusion of those living in cities that originated as Athenian colonies. In the Athenian view, this would include the Ionian cities of Asia Minor.

LYSISTRATA:

Then while we're still young and it's time to be living for
    pleasure,
we sleep by ourselves since our men are campaigning. I'm sorry
much less for myself than for girls getting old in their
    chambers.

COMMISSIONER:

Men also get old, do they not?

LYSISTRATA:

    But their cases are different.
Old soldiers wed children. The gray in their beards doesn't
    matter,
but the springtime of women is shorter. If one doesn't seize it,
a marriage is out of the question. She sits and she ponders.

COMMISSIONER:

If a guy can still get an erection . . .

LYSISTRATA:

What are you waiting for? Why not just die?
Here's space for the coffin that you'll need to buy.   600
And while I'm preparing a funeral cake,
here's change to pay Charon for crossing the lake.

OLD WOMAN 1:

And here are the ribbons we send with the dead.

OLD WOMAN 2:

And a lovely tiara to wear on your head.

LYSISTRATA:
Need anything else? For it's time to embark.
Lord Charon's inviting you into the dark.
You mustn't delay his departure!

COMMISSIONER:
How dare you shower me with such abuse?
The full commission's going to hear of this!
Just wait until they see what I've endured!   610

LYSISTRATA:
Unhappy that you didn't lie in state?
At break of day, the morning after next,
we'll celebrate your funeral in style.

> (COMMISSIONER exits via a side passage; LYSISTRATA
>   goes back into the Acropolis.)

MEN'S LEADER:
It's no time for freedom-loving citizens to sleep!
Let's take off our clothing, men, and make these women weep.

MEN'S CHORUS:
This situation has the stink
of higher aims. I fear
a tyranny like what we had
when Hippias[39] was here.

---

39. Hippias (hip´-pē-əs), Pisistratus' son, governed Athens as a tyrant
from his father's death in 527 BCE until his expulsion in 510.

It's obvious that Spartan men
convened at Cleisthenes's[40]   620
and cleverly prevailed upon
the women there to seize

money from the treasury,
the which I can't forgive.
It's funding for the jury-duty
fees I need to live!

MEN'S LEADER:

Gods! To think these women dare to give us men advice.
All they really know about is whether shields look nice.
Now they say that making peace with Sparta is a must.
Might as well maintain that drooling wolves deserve our
    trust!
Clearly what they're weaving now's a cloak for tyranny.   630
Never shall a gang of tyrants get the best of me!
I've unsheathed my dagger, which these myrtle blossoms hide
while I stand in armor at Aristogeiton's[41] side . . .

---

40. Cleisthenes (klīs´-thə-nēz), a contemporary Athenian frequently ridiculed on account of his effeminacy. He is not to be confused with the democratic statesman of the same name, the man responsible for the re-organization of Athens along democratic lines in 510 BCE.

41. An Athenian aristocrat, Aristogeiton (ə-ris´-tō-gī´-tən), and his lover Harmodius attempted to assassinate the tyrant Hippias in 514 BCE but only succeeded in killing his brother Hipparchus. Nevertheless, they were celebrated as the "tyrannicides" who liberated Athens from oppression. On the day of the attempted assassination, they and their fellow conspirators carried daggers hidden by myrtle branches. Statues representing Harmodius and Aristogeiton were erected in the agora. Thucydides (6.54.1–59.4) tells the whole story.

His statue's, that is.

. . . strike a noble pose like so, then leaping from my place,
smash that ancient, god-forsaken woman's ugly face.

WOMEN'S LEADER:
Back at home, you'll shock your mommy, bruised from toes to
  brow.

  (Beat.)

Time for action, female elders. Shed your jackets now!

  (Women choristers shed outer garments.)

WOMEN'S CHORUS:
Citizens of Athens, hear!
We've good advice to share.
In view of all you've done for us
to do so's only fair.   640

At the age of seven years,
I bore the mysteries.[42]
I ground our leader's grain[43] *at ten,*
and took off my chemise

42. Every year two noble girls were chosen to be *Arrhephoroi*. They re-
sided in the Acropolis, participating in various rituals including a secret
encounter with Aphrodite and Eros. The meaning of their title is unknown.
They are bearers (*phoroi*) of things called *arrhe-*, possibly standing for *arrheta*,
"unspoken" or "secret" things.

43. Our leader = Athena. Honey cakes were among the edibles offered
to the goddess.

to play the bear at Brauron[44] then,
and while the city prayed,
I marched with figs around my neck,
a basket-bearing maid.[45]

WOMEN'S LEADER:
Since the city's always been extraordinarily nice,
woman though I am, I'll give the state some good advice.
Don't be mad if I propose a novel stratagem.   650
I contribute something vital to this country: men.
Which of you pathetic geezers claim to offer more?
Squandering the properties grandfathers won in war?
You're exempt from taxes since you have no revenue.
We're confronting fiscal ruin all because of you.
Anything to say but "Grr"? Don't rile me up again.
If you do, I'll take this shoe and bust you in the chin.

MEN'S CHORUS:
Aren't speeches such as those   Strophe (659–681)
what "hubris" signifies?
What's worse they're growing bolder
before our very eyes!
We'd make them stop if we
had balls of any size.

44. Brauron (brȯ´-rən), a settlement on the east coast of Attica, had a small temple dedicated to Artemis. During its annual festival, the Brauronia, young girls, danced nude, imitating bears.

45. Noble maidens with unblemished reputations bore baskets in several kinds of procession. Like the baskets, fig necklaces symbolized agricultural abundance.

MEN'S LEADER:

Right! And take your tunics off. A man should smell like one.
Sausages in grape-leaf wrappers don't have any fun.

MEN'S CHORUS:

Yo white-footed men
who stormed Leipsydrium[46]
when we were still a thing,
the time to rise has come.

We have to fly again
and shake our bodies free
from head to toe of all
of age's misery.   670

MEN'S LEADER:

Right! For if we give the women here an inch or two,
there's no telling what their slimy hands will try to do.
Maybe build a fleet and launch a treacherous attack.
Persian Artemisia[47] was pretty good at that!
If they fight on horses, best to run away and hide.
Nothing beats a woman when it comes to "Mount and ride!"
Even at a gallop, Amazons will stick like glue.

---

46. Leipsydrium (ləp-sid´-rē-əm), the name of a fortress or hill in Attica.
It was the center of resistance to Hippias after the assassination of Hipparchus in 514 BCE. The fortress was captured by supporters of Hippias in 511.

47. Artemisia (är-tə-mē´-sē-ä), queen of Halicarnassus on the coast of
southeast Turkey. A subject and confidante of the Persian emperor, she
commanded a ship in the battle of Salamis during which she treacherously
rammed and sank another Persian vessel to avoid an Athenian attack. Cp.
Herodotus 8.87.88.

Mikon's[48] painting showing them in battle proves it true.
Evidently punishment is what these women need.   680
Grab them by their scrawny necks and have them pilloried.

WOMEN'S CHORUS:
If by the Holy Pair[49]   Antistrophe (681–695)
your actions bother me,
I'll let my anger loose,
I'll set my wild boar free.
"Oh help me, friends!" you'll cry,
in total misery.

WOMEN'S LEADER:
Ladies, let's take off our cloaks. It's time to go unclad.
Give these men a whiff of angry women fighting mad.   690

WOMEN'S CHORUS:
If someone hits me now,
his use of teeth is past.
No chewing beans or garlic.
He'll face a total fast.

Don't you dare insult me.
I won't take any crap.
If you're the eagle's egg,
I'm shit on Zeus's lap.[50]

48. Mikon (mē´-kən), a renowned painter of the mid-fifth century BCE.
49. Demeter and her daughter Persephone.
50. A reference to *Aesop's Fables* 3. Feuding with an eagle, a dung beetle keeps rolling the eagle's eggs out of its nest. To safeguard the eggs, the eagle finally places them on Zeus' lap. The dung beetle rolls a ball of dung next to them. Seeing it, Zeus jumps to his feet, inadvertently breaking the eggs.

WOMEN'S LEADER:
Men aren't going to worry me while Lampito survives,
she and dear Ismenia, those noble Grecian wives.
You won't ever bring those lovely women to their knees—
hated widely as you are—by passing new decrees.
Yesterday I meant to give my young girlfriends a feast.   700
I invited foreigners, among them not the least
Miss Boeotian Eel, a dearly loved and skillful maid.
I was told she couldn't come because your laws forbade.
It's apparent you won't cease from passing them until
someone grabs you by the leg and oops! A fatal spill!

(Enter LYSISTRATA from the Acropolis. Beat.)

WOMEN'S CHORUS:
Hail sovereign queen revered in thought and deed!
What does your angry countenance portend?

LYSISTRATA:
The things that wicked women think and do
have left me pacing back and forth depressed.

WOMEN'S LEADER:
What are you saying? What?   710

LYSISTRATA:
The truth, that's all.

WOMEN'S LEADER:
And what's this awful truth? Inform your friends!

LYSISTRATA:
To speak is shameful; keeping silent, hard.

WOMEN'S LEADER:
Don't hide the truth, however bad, from me!

LYSISTRATA:
We're desperate to—to be concise—get laid.

WOMEN'S LEADER:
O Zeus!

LYSISTRATA:
    Why call on Zeus? The problem's this.
I can't control the women anymore.
They're always running off to be with men.
I caught the first deserter over there,   720
drilling a hole beside the cave of Pan;[51]
another going down on ropes attached
to pulleys. One aboard a sparrow's back[52]
was heading for Orsilochus's[53] house.
I caught her by the hair just yesterday.
There's no excuse so lame it's not been tried.

---

51. A small cave on the side of the Acropolis.
52. Sparrow was one of many slang terms for penis. Some vase paintings depicted women riding birds whose beaks were phallus shaped.
53. Nothing is known about Orsilochus (ər-siˊ-lə-kəs) except what can be inferred from this text; his house had a bad reputation.

(WIFE 1 hurries out of the Acropolis gates.)

But look! There's one of them approaching now.
Hey you there, what's the rush?

WIFE 1:
    I must go home.
I have some coverlets, Milesian wool.
The moths are killing them.

LYSISTRATA:
    What savage moths!   730
Go back the way you came!

WIFE 1:
    I won't be long.
I'll spread the wool across my bed, that's all.

LYSISTRATA:
No spreading wool or going anywhere!

WIFE 1:
And let my wool be ruined?

LYSISTRATA:
    If you must.

    (LYSISTRATA chases WIFE 1 back through the Acropolis
        gate. As she exits, WIFE 2 emerges.)

WIFE 2:

Oh sorry, sorry me! It slipped my mind
somehow to shuck my flax.[54]

LYSISTRATA:

   Another one!
She's boldly going forth to shuck her flax!
Hey! Turn around!

WIFE 2:

   By Aphrodite, please!
Just let me shuck my flax and come right back.

LYSISTRATA:

No shucking flax! Since once you've started that,   740
the other wives will soon be shucking theirs.

(As WIFE 2 exits through the Acropolis gate, WIFE 3
   emerges. Her belly looks swollen, as though she is in the
   final month of pregnancy.)

WIFE 3:

O lady Eileithyia,[55] please delay
my child until I reach a hallowed spot.

LYSISTRATA:

Now what's your problem?

---

54. Shuck my flax: Henderson's brilliant translation. See his Loeb translation, ll. 735–741.

55. Eileithyia (ā-lā´-thē-ä), a goddess associated with childbirth, invoked by women in labor.

WIFE 3:
Labor pains. Severe.

LYSISTRATA:
But you weren't pregnant yesterday!

WIFE 3:
Today
I am. Please send me home, Lysistrata.
I need a midwife now!

LYSISTRATA:
Oh really? Why?
What have we here?

(LYSISTRATA feels her belly, then taps it with her fist. This
produces a metallic noise.)

It's hard.

WIFE 3:
I have a son!

LYSISTRATA:
By Aphrodite, it's becoming clear   750
that what you have is hollow bronze. Let's see . . .

(LYSISTRATA uncovers a large, bronze helmet.)

Athena's helmet! *This* is what you called
your unborn child.

WIFE 3:

  I'm really pregnant though!

LYSISTRATA:

Then what's the helmet for?

WIFE 3:

  If I give birth
on the Acropolis I'll lay the babe
inside the helmet like a nesting dove.

LYSISTRATA:

Enough of these absurd excuses, please!
Stay here until your helmet's naming day.   760

WIFE 3:

I simply cannot go to sleep up there,
not since I saw the snake that guards the place.[56]

WIFE 4 (entering hurriedly from the Acropolis gate):
That's it! I'm dead. The owls are killing me
with constant hooting. Who could fall asleep?

LYSISTRATA:

Dear ladies! Stop exaggerating now.
Perhaps you miss your husbands. Don't you know
that they are missing you? Their nights are hard.

---

56. The statue of Athena in the Parthenon and other representations of
Athena showed a giant serpent coiled at her feet. Pious Athenians appar-
ently believed that a real serpent guarded the Parthenon.

Of that I'm very sure. We must endure!
We must persist a little more. I have
an oracle predicting victory
provided we avoid internal strife.

(LYSISTRATA removes a small scroll from her bosom.)

WIVES 3 and 4:
Say what it says!

LYSISTRATA:
   Just quiet down! I will.

"When cowering swallows assemble, concealed in a single
      redoubt,   770
afraid of the well-crested hoopoe, and phallus-wise doing
      without,
there will come a cessation of evil; for Zeus, the great god of
      the sky,
will lower the higher and heighten the lower."

WIVES 3 and 4:
We'll lay on the top, you and I!

LYSISTRATA:
"If the swallows descend to dissension and fly on their wings
      far away,
leaving their holy enclosure, no creature is shameless as they."

WIVES 3 and 4:
The meaning of that oracle is clear!

LYSISTRATA:
Let's not renounce our plans from weakness then,
but settle down within. To disrespect
an oracle's a shameful thing to do.   780

  (LYSISTRATA and WIVES 3 and 4 exit through the
     Acropolis gate. The MEN'S CHORUS rises to sing and
     dance, addressing the WOMEN'S CHORUS.)

MEN'S CHORUS:
There is a certain narrative
I'd like to share with you.
I heard it as a youthful lad,
and it concerns one too.

The boy was named Melanion
and his distinction this:
he hated marriage so much that
he sought the wilderness.[57]

He and his dog up in the hills
spread nets where rabbits roam   790
He hated women so much that
he never came back home.

Oh yes, he hated women but,
when all is said and done,
we, the wise, despise them more
than good Melanion.

57. Cp. Apollodorus 3.9.6 for the story of Melanion (mə-laˊ-nē-ən). The
old men suppress the detail that he was the companion and eventual husband of the lovely Atalanta.

MEN'S LEADER:
Grandmother, hey! How 'bout a kiss?

WOMEN'S LEADER (averting her face, disgusted):
Onions, whew! Leave them alone!

MEN'S LEADER:
Well then, I'll kick your butt like this.

   (MEN'S LEADER executes a mule kick in the direction of
     WOMEN'S LEADER.)

WOMEN'S LEADER:
My! What an awesome bush you've grown!   800

MEN'S LEADER:
Myronides[58] was hairy there,
a real bad ass to enemies,
and one could argue pubic hair
made Phormio[59] a Heracles.

WOMEN'S CHORUS:
I also have a tale to tell
and when my telling's done,
you'll have a paradigm to set
against Melanion.

---

58. Myronides (mī-rä´-ni-dēz), an Athenian general famous for leading
a reserve army of youths and elders to victory over a Corinthian force
around 458 BCE.

59. Phormio (fər´-mē-ō), an Athenian general remembered for naval
victories in the Corinthian Gulf early in the Peloponnesian War.

Now Timon[60] was a vagabond,
a splinter off the Furies' block.   810
All his thorny tongue could do
was criticize and mock.

His hatred was so great he fled
the company of men.
He cursed them all and disappeared
and wasn't seen again.

Like us he hated wicked men
more than words can tell,
which is no doubt the reason why
we women loved him well.   820

WOMEN'S LEADER:
Should I punch you? Yes or no?

MEN'S LEADER (sarcastically):
I'm so afraid. Please don't, I pray.

WOMEN'S LEADER:
Or I could kick your butt like so.

MEN'S LEADER:
And put your pussy on display?

---

60. Timon (tī´-mən), a legendary Athenian misanthrope. Aristophanes is the earliest author to refer to him. Cp. also Plutarch's *Antony* 70 and Lucian's *Timon.*

WOMEN'S LEADER:
You wouldn't see a single thing.
I may be looking old and beat
but I've sufficient carpeting
and use a lamp to keep it neat.[61]

>   (The choruses and their leaders relax. KINESIAS enters via a
>   side passage. He is in pain and sports a giant erection. He is
>   followed by a slave, MANES, carrying an infant.
>   LYSISTRATA appears on the Acropolis wall.)

LYSISTRATA:
Hey ho! What's this? I need some women here
and quickly.

OLD WOMAN 1 (appearing beside LYSISTRATA):
  What's the matter? What's the fuss?   830

LYSISTRATA:
A man's approaching, terribly distraught.
He's caught in Aphrodite's mystic net.
O Paphian and Cytherean queen![62]
O Cypriot! Keep marching straight ahead!

OLD WOMAN 1:
Who's he and where's he at?

---

61. Possibly an actual practice. Cp. *Thesmophoriazusae* 236–249 for a
comical dramatization. The usual Greek lamp looked like a covered gravy
boat containing olive oil with a spout from which a small flame shone.

62. Cythera (si-thē´-rə), according to Hesiod (*Theogony* 192), Aphrodite came to life in the foam of the sea as she floated past this island en route
to Cyprus.

LYSISTRATA:
By Chloe's shrine.[63]

OLD WOMAN 1:
I see him now, by Zee! Who is he though?

LYSISTRATA:
A man that someone here must surely know.

MYRTLE (appearing beside LYSISTRATA):
I do! He married me! Kinesias!

LYSISTRATA:
Then it's your job to roast and torture him.
Befuddle him with love and its reverse.   840
Grant everything but what the wine cup knows.

MYRTLE:
Don't worry. I can handle that.

LYSISTRATA:
    Okay!
I'll stay to help deceive and blister him.
The rest of you, lie low a little while.

(The other women withdraw to the Acropolis. MYRTLE and
    LYSISTRATA stay. KINESIAS is now squarely in front of
    the Acropolis gates.)

63. Chloe (klō´-ē), "the Green One," another name for Demeter. According to Pausanias (1.22.3) there was a shrine to Demeter Chloe on an approach
to Acropolis.

KINESIAS:
Ah me! What wrenching, wracking pain I'm in!
I might as well be shackled to a wheel!

LYSISTRATA:
Who's that who penetrates our guard?

KINESIAS:
  It' me.

LYSISTRATA:
A man?

KINESIAS:
  Indeed.

LYSISTRATA:
  Then kindly go away.

KINESIAS:
And who's it throws me out?

LYSISTRATA:
  The daytime guard.

KINESIAS:
By god, good guard, call Myrtle here to me!   850

LYSISTRATA (mocking KINESIAS):
"Call Myrtle here to me!" And who are you?

KINESIAS:
Her man, Kinesias Paeonides.[64]

LYSISTRATA:
Why dearest friend, hello! Your name is not
unknown to us, but quite the opposite.
In fact, it's always on your woman's lips.
Before she eats an egg or any fruit
she says, "To my Kinesias!"

KINESIAS:
  O gods!

LYSISTRATA:
I swear by Aphrodite! When there's talk
of men, your woman doesn't hesitate.
Compared to mine, she says, the rest are rot.   860

KINESIAS:
Go get her please!

LYSISTRATA:
  Got anything for me?

KINESIAS:
You bet I do, if you're amenable.

---

64. Kinesias of the Paeonidae (pē-ə´-ni-dē) deme. Since Cleisthenes' reforms, Athenians were known by their deme's name instead of their father's
names.

(KINESIAS raises his tunic to expose his erection.
LYSISTRATA recoils in disgust.)

LYSISTRATA:
Gach!

(Getting the message, KINESIAS rearranges his tunic and
extracts a small purse.)

Well then there's this. It's all I have. It's yours.

(He tosses the purse to LYSISTRATA.)

LYSISTRATA:
Okay. I'm getting Myrtle.

KINESIAS:
Quickly please!

(Soliloquizing.)

There isn't any pleasure left in life
since Myrtle left our cozy little home.
Now entering its doorway causes pain
for everything seems cold and empty. Food
has lost its taste—and oh! My stiffy throbs!

MYRTLE (unseen, from inside the Acropolis):
I love him, yes I do! The problem's this: 870
he doesn't want my love. Don't make me go!

KINESIAS:
Sweet little Myrtle-wertle, what's the deal?
Come down!

MYRTLE (appearing above the Acropolis gate):
    Not me, by Zee! Down there? No way!

KINESIAS:
It's me who's calling you! Why disobey?

MYRTLE:
Since you don't really want me after all.

KINESIAS:
Not *want* you? No. I *need* you desperately.

MYRTLE:
Goodbye.

KINESIAS:
    No wait! You can't ignore your child.
You there! It's time to call your mommy now.

CHILD:
Mommy! Mommy! Mommy!

KINESIAS:
What's with you, woman? Don't you pity him?   880
He's gone a week without being fed or washed.

MYRTLE:
I pity him when I observe how cruel
his father is.

KINESIAS:
　Come down and see him, witch!

MYRTLE:
That's motherhood! One must go down.

　(MYRTLE disappears behind the wall en route to the gate.
　　KINESIAS soliloquizes.)

KINESIAS:
　Ah me!
I'd swear that she's a younger woman now.
She has a sweeter, gentler kind of look.
Even her bitchiness and arrogance
stir sweet desires fit to break my heart.

MYRTLE (emerging from the gate and hurrying to her child):
O sweetest child your evil father bred!　　　　　　　890
Come here and let me kiss you, darling babe.

KINESIAS:
What's wrong with you, provoking me like this,
obeying those other women, hurting me?
You'll soon be sorry.

MYRTLE:
　Don't you touch me, dear.

KINESIAS:

Your management of household goods, both yours
and mine, has gone to hell.

MYRTLE:

As though I cared!

KINESIAS:

You're not concerned that hens are ruining
your woolies?

MYRTLE:

No. That doesn't bother me.

KINESIAS:

And Aphrodite's rites? It's been so long
since we've observed them. Aren't you coming home?

MYRTLE:

Not till you men resolve your differences
and end the war.

900

KINESIAS:

Okay, when that seems best,
that's what we'll do.

MYRTLE:

Okay, and when you do,
I'll head for home. For now, I'm sworn to stay.

KINESIAS:
Well then lie down with me a little while.

MYRTLE:
No! Though I do admit to loving you.

KINESIAS:
Then Myrtle, why refuse to lie with me?

MYRTLE:
Don't be ridiculous! Our child's right there.

KINESIAS:
For god's sake, Manes, take the kid away.

>   (MANES picks up the child and scrambles out of sight via a
>   side passage. KINESIAS turns back to MYRTLE.)

Alright, the little brat's no longer here.
Now come and lie with me!

MYRTLE:
    But where can we   910
lie down, poor dear?

KINESIAS:
    Pan's grotto would be nice.

MYRTLE:
I'll be impure. I won't be welcomed back.

KINESIAS:
No problem. You can bathe in Clepsydra.[65]

MYRTLE:
But still I'll have to break my sacred vow.

KINESIAS:
That's on my head. Don't give it any thought.

MYRTLE:
Well then, I better get a bed.

KINESIAS:
   Please don't.
The ground suffices.

MYRTLE:
   Lord Apollo, no!
You mustn't lie in dirt, you foolish man.

   (MYRTLE runs into the Acropolis).

KINESIAS:
She truly loves me. *That* is crystal clear.

   (MYRTLE returns with a cot made of leather straps on a
     wooden frame.)

65. Clepsydra (klep´-sü-dra), the name of a fountain at the northern
base of the Acropolis, also a common noun meaning "water clock."

MYRTLE:
Now settle down on this while I undress.   920
But wait! I have to get a mattress first!

KINESIAS:
A mattress? Nah.

MYRTLE:
   Oh yes, by Artemis!
Real gentlemen don't sleep on straps.

KINESIAS:
   Kiss kiss?

MYRTLE:
There, there!

   (She gives him a quick kiss and rushes back into the
      Acropolis.)

KINESIAS:
   Oh god! I'm desperate. Hurry back!

   (MYRTLE reenters from the Acropolis with a mattress.)

MYRTLE:
Your mattress, sir. Now rest while I undress.
But wait! No pillows? That won't do at all!

KINESIAS:
But I don't want a pillow.

MYRTLE:
It's for me.

(MYRTLE exits to get a pillow.)

KINESIAS (petting his erection):
My boy's like Heracles at dinnertime.

MYRTLE (returning with pillows, which she arranges on the
    bed behind KINESIAS):
Sit up. Lean forward.

(KINESIAS obeys, then lies back down with pillows behind
    his neck and shoulders.)

All is ready now.

KINESIAS (nodding toward his erection):
Oh yes! It truly is, my golden girl.   930

MYRTLE:
My breastband's almost off. Remember now,
you gave your solemn word concerning peace.

KINESIAS:
By Zee! I swear!

MYRTLE:
What's this? No sleeping gown!

KINESIAS:
Which I don't need. I need to copulate.

MYRTLE:
And so you shall. Don't worry. I'll be back.

(MYRTLE heads back to the Acropolis.)

KINESIAS:
She's killing me with woolen merchandise.

(MYRTLE returns from the Acropolis with a sleeping gown.)

MYRTLE:
Now up we go!

KINESIAS (nodding toward his erection):
I'm up already. See!

MYRTLE:
How 'bout some perfume?

KINESIAS:
By Apollo, no!

MYRTLE:
You have to try some. Aphrodite says.

(MYRTLE runs into the Acropolis to get some perfume.)

KINESIAS:
Lord Zeus, I only pray she spills it all. 940

MYRTLE (returning with a round bottle):
I'm back! Give me your hand. Now rub some on.

KINESIAS:
I don't approve this scent. I catch the whiff
of more delays, not that of married bliss.

MYRTLE:
O silly me! I brought the stuff from Rhodes!

KINESIAS:
It's fine. Don't worry so!

MYRTLE:
    That's crazy talk!

    (MYRTLE runs into the Acropolis for more perfume.)

KINESIAS:
May perfume's first inventor die in pain!

MYRTLE (returning with a cylindrical container):
Here try this alabaster tube.

KINESIAS (nodding in the usual direction):
    I've got
my own. Lie down, you wretched girl. Don't bring
another thing.

MYRTLE:

    Your wish is my command.
    I'm taking off my shoes. Oh, by the way . . .   950

    (MYRTLE tiptoes toward the Acropolis, unseen by
       KINESIAS.)

    . . . you won't forget to vote for peace?

    (MYRTLE dashes through the Acropolis gates that close
      behind her.)

KINESIAS:

    We'll see.

    (Turning, KINESIAS discovers that MYRTLE is gone.)

She's murdered me! She crushed my corpse to bits
and skinned the parts! And now she's gone away.

Alas! I've no one now to screw!
I've lost the love of one most fair.
How can I soothe my thing? Eheu!
O pimps, I need some tender care!

MEN'S LEADER:

Poor wreck, you're in a frightful state!
Being so deceived you've gone insane.   960
All I can do's commiserate.
How can your kidneys stand the pain?

How can your balls and soul endure?
How your bulging groin? Your back?
How those sexless mornings? (Brr!)
Your bed's become a steely rack!

KINESIAS:
Oh god! These cramps are killing me!

MEN'S LEADER:
And she's the cause of your distress.
She's evil to the nth degree.

KINESIAS:
Yes, she's my sweet, my loveliness!   970

MEN'S LEADER:
No, you boob! An evil bitch!

KINESIAS:
One or both, I don't know which.

Zeus hurl her heavenward I pray
like haystacks in a hurricane
and once you've carried her away
drop her toward the Attic Plain.

Let her traverse the space between us
and land right on my throbbing . . . member.

(Beat. The SPARTAN HERALD enters via a side passage.)

SPARTAN HERALD:
Where do thine elder counselors convene—   980
thy so-called prytaneis?[66] I've news to share.

KINESIAS:
And you are what? Priapus? Hominid?

SPARTAN HERALD:
A Spartan herald, thou contentious bug.
I come anent negotiating peace.

KINESIAS (pointing to the herald's erection):
And that, I guess, explains your hidden spear.

SPARTAN HERALD:
I've no such weapon.

KINESIAS:
    Stop! Don't turn away!
Why close your cloak like that? Perhaps your groin
is swollen from your trip?

SPARTAN HERALD:
    Rave on, by Twins!

KINESIAS (exposing the herald's erection):
Aha! You've got a giant stiffy there!

66. Prytaneis (prī´-tə-nāz), men chosen by lot to serve on the Council
of 500, which was the executive committee of the assembly of all citizens.
Each of ten groups of fifty prytaneis served for one tenth of a year.

SPARTAN HERALD:
Not I, by Zeus! Arrest thy blabbering! 990

KINESIAS:
Then what is *that*?

SPARTAN HERALD:
 A Spartan skytalé.[67]

KINESIAS (baring his erection):
If so, I've got one too. Here, check it out!

 (Beat.)

But honestly, I'm not a fool; so tell
the truth. What's happening in Sparta now?

SPARTAN HERALD:
All Sparta hath extreme rigidity.
Her allies have it very hard as well.

KINESIAS:
And what's the cause of said calamity?
The goat god Pan?

SPARTAN HERALD:
 'Twas Lampito at first.
Then other women, everywhere in Greece,

 67. Skytalé (skī´-tə-lē), an ingenious device for sending coded messages.
See note 10 in the introduction.

as though a single signal set them free,   1000
refused to let us stroke their hystakones.[68]

KINESIAS:
How are you coping?

SPARTAN HERALD:
  Wretchedly forsooth!
We slouch like windswept fools with flick'ring lamps.
Our women won't permit us e'en to touch
their myrtle blossoms till with one accord
we make a treaty bringing Hellas peace.

KINESIAS:
Behind this lies a great conspiracy
by women. That's becoming obvious.

  (Beat.)

Return to Sparta! Bid the elders there
to send a delegation authorized   1010
to end the war. I'll beg our councilors
to do the same. . . . I'll even show them this.

  (He exposes his erection.)

SPARTAN HERALD:
I'm off! Thine urgency rebukes delay.

    68. Hystakones: a Greek word of unknown meaning, used metaphori-
cally here.

(The SPARTAN HERALD exits by the way he came.)

MEN'S LEADER:
Nothing beats a woman when it comes to getting mad.
No beast or fire equals her. No leopard's half as bad.

WOMEN'S LEADER:
Knowing that, you still insist, you fool, on making war,
even though you'd find in me a faithful friend and more.

MEN'S LEADER:
That's because misogyny is rather slow to die.

WOMEN'S LEADER:
Take your time. Meanwhile we're glimpsing all too much of you.
If you really want to look ridiculous—you do.   1020
Let me join you over there and help you with your shirt.

    (WOMEN'S LEADER helps him put his shirt on. The lady
      choristers assist their male counterparts.)

MEN'S LEADER:
Thanks for helping me so kindly with that little chore.
Boiling anger made me drop my clothing on the floor.

WOMEN'S LEADER:
Now you look more like the kind of man I'd like to hug.
If you hadn't been so nasty, I'd have caught the bug[69]
feasting on your sorry eyeball even as we speak.

69. This passage seems to imply the existence of a saying in which having a bug in the eye stands for anger. Here Aristophanes brings such a saying to life in a surrealistic manner.

MEN'S LEADER:
That's what makes my eyeball itchy! Kindly take this ring,
scrape my eye, remove the bug, and let me see the thing.
It's been chewing on my eye as long I recall.

WOMEN'S LEADER:
I'll perform this chore for you although you call me "slut."   1030

> (She scrapes the eye of the MEN'S LEADER as promised
> and extracts a large insect.)

Gods! Was that a giant gnat infesting you or what!
Take a look. I'd say it's from the swamps of Marathon.

MEN'S LEADER:
Thanks a lot! That bug's been drilling holes in me for years.
Now it's been removed by you, my eyes are bathed in tears!

WOMEN'S LEADER:
Come, I'll wipe your tears away, you wicked, wicked man,
wipe your tears and kiss your lips.

MEN'S LEADER:
    You can't!

WOMEN'S LEADER:
    Oh yes I can!

> (WOMEN'S LEADER kisses him on the lips.)

MEN'S LEADER:
Stop that stuff! You're acting like a silly prostitute!

(MEN'S LEADER's anger is decreasing because of the kiss.)

There's an ancient proverb, true and eloquent to boot.
It maintains you cannot live with women or without.

(His anger melts completely.)

Yet will I make peace with you so there can be no doubt   1040
that I'll never do to you (or you to me) a wrong.
All together, now begin! Join hands and sing a song!

UNIFIED CHORUS:
Don't think that we will now begin   Strophe (1043–1057)
abusing some poor citizen.
That isn't what the city needs.
Instead we have kind words and deeds.
The evil acts we could decry
will still be with us by and by.
Let's hear the voices, his and hers,
of our impoverished commoners.   1050
Are you lacking two or three
minas?[70] Simply come to me.
I've got the money. Purses too.
When peace returns and hopes renew,
we shall abolish all the debt
of those who borrowed. Sure, you bet!

(The chorus laughs heartily at their own joke.)

---

70. One mina = 100 drachmas. One drachma was a rower's daily wage.

I'm obliged to wine and dine   Antistrophe (1058–1071)
some rich Euboean friends of mine.   1060
Thick soup is boiling in the pot.
And there's the suckling pig I got,
I roasted it with special care.
Its meat is sweet and tender fare.
Now here's a thought. Why don't you pay
a visit to my house today?
Bathe and bring your children too.
Walk right up without ado.
Even look a little bored.
Imitate a haughty lord
entering his mansion, but   1070
you'll find the door is bolted shut.

(More choral laughter. Enter the SPARTAN
    DELEGATES.)

MEN'S LEADER (addressing the UNIFIED CHORUS):
Unless I'm mistaken, these creatures are elders from Sparta.
I judge by their beards and the pigs that their robes are concealing.

(To the Spartans.)

For starters, men of Lacedaemon, hail!
And second tell us how you're faring now.

SPARTAN DELEGATE:
Why needest thou a plenitude of words?
Thine eyes inform thee how we're faring now.

(The Spartans expose their erections.)

MEN'S LEADER:
Good gods! Such tension looks unbearable.
Your inflammation's getting worse and worse.

SPARTAN DELEGATE:
Why speak anent unspeakable distress?   1080
Let someone hasten hitherward with peace!

(Enter the ATHENIAN DELEGATES. All are
    crouching.)

MEN'S LEADER:
Well timed! Behold! Our delegates are here.
Note how they crouch like wrestlers set to fight.
That posture gives their cloaks some needed room.
Each has an ugly case of athlete's putz.

FIRST ATHENIAN DELEGATE (addressing MEN'S
    LEADER):
Where does Lysistrata hold court? As you
can see, we're men. Our case is similar.

(The Athenians expose their erections.)

MEN'S LEADER:
There is a certain similarity.
Do you have spasms near the break of day?

FIRST ATHENIAN DELEGATE:
And how! We're totally exhausted, man.   1090
If we don't have a treaty pretty soon
we're gonna end up doing Cleisthenes!

MEN'S LEADER:
I think you'd better buckle up your cloaks.
Some drunken reveler[71] might catch sight of you.

FIRST ATHENIAN DELEGATE:
That sounds like good advice.

(The Athenians cover their erections.)

SPARTAN ELDER:
    Aye, verily!
'Tis excellent advice in every way.

(The Spartans cover their erections.)

FIRST ATHENIAN DELEGATE:
Dear Spartans! Gods! How we've been suffering!

SPARTAN DELEGATE:
Sweet chucks, we too have suffered horribly.
Methinks these fellows seen us masturbate.

FIRST ATHENIAN DELEGATE:
There, there, relax and tell us everything.   1100
What brings you here?

SPARTAN DELEGATE:
    We're delegates in search
of peace.

71. In 415, on the eve of the Sicilian expedition, vandals mutilated ithy-
phallic statues of Hermes.

FIRST ATHENIAN DELEGATE:

Well, well! Our goals are similar.
Let's get Lysistrata, for she's unique.
Through her alone can we be reconciled.

SPARTAN DELEGATE:
Lysistrata, Lysistratus—who cares?[72]

FIRST ATHENIAN DELEGATE:
She doesn't need a summons, so it seems.
She evidently heard us. Here she comes.

(Enter LYSISTRATA from the Acropolis.)

UNIFIED CHORUS:
All hail the most manly of women! It's time to be forceful
but flexible, uppity, lowly, majestic but friendly,
broadminded. The princes of Greece have succumbed
   to your magic.   1110
They jointly request that you settle their longstanding quarrel.

LYSISTRATA:
No problem *if* they're really seeking peace,
not poking one another's weaknesses.
But where did Reconciliation go?

(Enter from the Acropolis a naked girl, RECONCILIATION
    personified.)

72. I.e., "Woman or man, what's the difference?"

Ah! Now the Spartans—bring them here to me.
No heavy-handed, rough-stuff though. No force.
Don't act the way our foolish husbands do.
Employ your gentle femininity.
If one won't take your hand, then grab his balls.
Come on and bring those men of Athens too.   1120
Use any body part that's sticking out.
Okay. Now Spartans stand beside me here.
You other fellows there and hear me well.
A woman though I am, I have a mind.
My mental faculties are unimpaired
and often having heard my elders speak,
I've had the best of educations too.
I have some things to say to both of you,
some just rebukes. You share a single cup
at Delphi's shrine, The Gates, Olympia,[73]   1130
and other sacred places I could name.
With armed barbarians nearby, you choose
to kill your fellow Greeks and wreck their states.
Part one of my oration's now complete.

FIRST ATHENIAN DELEGATE (staring at
    RECONCILIATION):
My stiffy's in an awful state alright!

73. Delphi's shrine is Apollo's famous oracular temple; Thermopylae,
"The Hot Gates" in Greek, the site of famous stand of the three hundred
Spartans against the Persians; Olympia, site of the original Olympics in the
northwest Peloponnesus.

LYSISTRATA:

And now the Spartans. Let's consider you.
Do you recall when Perikleidas[74] came,
the pale-faced Spartan cloaked in red? He sat   1140
in supplication here and begged for help
because Messenia was in revolt[75]
and god was shaking up the Spartan earth?
So Kimon[76] led four thousand hoplites there
and Lacedaemon, thanks to him, was saved!
Now in return for Athens's noble act
you're set on ravaging her countryside.

FIRST ATHENIAN DELEGATE:

That clearly isn't fair, Lysistrata!

SPARTAN DELEGATE (looking at RECONCILIATION):

And yet . . . good god! Her derriere's sublime!

LYSISTRATA:

Don't think I'll let you men of Athens off!
Remember how the Spartans rescued you   1150
when you were dressed in wooly peasant frocks?
They killed a thousand men of Thessaly

74. Perikleidas (per´-ə-klā´-dəs) is otherwise unknown. From this passage, he seems to have been a Spartan general or ambassador. That Athena
calls him pale-faced implies that he was fearful. Spartans wore red cloaks.

75. On the Messenian revolt, see note 6 in the introduction.

76. Kimon (kī´-mən), famous Athenian statesman and general, best
known for destroying a Persian fleet and army at the Battle of Eurymedon,
ca. 466 BCE. His attempt to help the Spartans defeat the Messenian revolt
was actually rebuffed by the Spartans.

together with the friends of Hippias.[77]
They cast them out alone that happy day
and freed the state. Instead of wooly frocks,
you started wearing finely woven robes.

SPARTAN DELEGATE (still looking at RECONCILIATION):
Ne'er have I gazed on anyone more fair.

FIRST ATHENIAN DELEGATE (also staring):
I've never seen a more inviting cave.

LYSISTRATA:
It seems we've made a good beginning here.
What's ever gained by war? Why don't you stop?   1160
Why not be reconciled? What's in the way?

SPARTAN DELEGATE:
With one concession we'll comply, to wit:
this mound.

    (He is treating RECONCILIATION's body like a map of
      Greece.)

LYSISTRATA:

    Which mound?

77. In 510 BCE Spartan troops defeated the forces of Hippias, tyrant of Athens, and his Thessalian allies, thus paving the way for the adoption of a democratic constitution in Athens. Lysistrata implies that the Athenians were so poor under Hippias that they wore sheepskins.

SPARTAN ELDER:

The mound called Pylos. Here!
We've loved and fondled it for oh so long!

FIRST ATHENIAN DELEGATE:

No by Poseidon! You're not getting that.

LYSISTRATA:

Oh let it go!

FIRST ATHENIAN DELEGATE:

Then who'll be left to screw?

LYSISTRATA:

Just ask for something else you'd like to have.

FIRST ATHENIAN DELEGATE (pointing to various parts
of RECONCILIATION):

Echinous,[78] home to porcupines, the gulf
of Malea, the legs of Megara.   1170

SPARTAN DELEGATE:

Nay! By the twain, not all of them! Forbear!

LYSISTRATA:

Come on, you two, don't argue over legs!

---

78. Echinous (e-kē´-nüs), a small town in northern Greece. Its name
is derived from the Greek word *echinus*, for porcupines and other prickly
creatures.

FIRST ATHENIAN DELEGATE (suddenly an enthusiastic
    convert, still drooling at RECONCILIATION):
I'm hot to strip and plow my acres nude!

SPARTAN DELEGATE (same as the Athenian):
Come dawn, I'll spread thick oxen shit o'er mine.

LYSISTRATA:
Once you've become each other's friends, you shall,
but first you must achieve a settlement.
You should consult your loyal allies too.

FIRST ATHENIAN DELEGATE:
What allies? Things are way too hard for that!
Our friends are all agreed on what we need.
It's sex!

SPARTAN DELEGATE:
    Decrees to such effect shall please   1180
our allies too!

FIRST ATHENIAN DELEGATE:
    And our Euboean guests.

LYSISTRATA:
Well said! Stay pure a little longer now.
We women have a feast for you above.

    (She points to the Acropolis gates.)

We've ample food in baskets brought from home.
While dining, swear that you'll be faithful friends.
Then each of you may grab your proper wife
and scurry home.

FIRST ATHENIAN DELEGATE:
   So let's get going now!

SPARTAN DELEGATE:
Aye! Thither away!

FIRST ATHENIAN DELEGATE:
   No time to waste! Come on!

   (All exit into the Acropolis. They are understood to be
     feasting there while the chorus performs.)

UNIFIED CHORUS:
Golden trinkets, linens, and
ornamental tapestries,
full-length robes for looking grand,   1190
I'd gladly give you all of these
for you to give your sons to use
or should somebody's daughter be
the one the sovereign people choose
to bear a basket, come to me.
Help yourself to all I've got
inside my house. Take what you please.
No seal's so strong that it cannot
be dusted off and cracked with ease.
Search high and low. Let torches shine.

Take what you find and have a ball.   1200
Unless your eyesight out-sees mine,
you won't find anything at all!

    (Again, the choristers all laugh at their own joke.)

Is anybody out of bread
and has a flock of slaves to feed
or lots of little kids instead?
I'd gladly give you all you need.
My grain is finely ground. That's why
you get a loaf from every cup.
If you're a poor man don't be shy,   1210
bring a sack and step right up.
My servant Manes, he'll be there.
Present your sack and have him pour
all you need, but please take care
when you approach the big front door.
Stop before you get too near,
at where I post a catalog
of dos and don'ts and things to fear.
Especially this: "Beware of dog!"

    (More laughter by the choristers. During the songs, a
        small group of slaves has gathered on stage and lounge
        around in front the Acropolis gate. Perhaps they are
        hoping for scraps from the feast. The drunken, torch-
        bearing FIRST ATHENIAN DELEGATE and the
        other ATHENIAN DELEGATES, having feasted, want
        to leave the Acropolis, but their way is blocked by the
        slaves.)

FIRST ATHENIAN DELEGATE (speaking from behind the
    closed doorway):
Hey fellows! Open up! You're in our way.
What made you choose to sit down there? Perhaps
you want to feel my torch? That old cliché!
I couldn't sink so low!

    (Beat.)

    Oh what the hell!
I'll go to any length to please the crowd.   1220

    (The FIRST ATHENIAN DELEGATE sticks his torch
        under the gate. The slaves scatter to avoid the flames. The
        chorus laughs. The FIRST ATHENIAN DELEGATE
        pushes his way through the gates and enters accompanied
        by the other ATHENIAN DELEGATES. All carry
        torches.)

SECOND ATHENIAN DELEGATE:
I'll also go to any length for you!

    (To the slaves.)

Get out of here or tell your hair goodbye.

    (He chases a slave offstage with his torch, nearly igniting his
        hair. The chorus laughs some more.)

FIRST ATHENIAN DELEGATE:
Get out and let the Spartans dine and leave
without encountering the likes of you.

SECOND ATHENIAN DELEGATE:
What a superior symposium!
The Spartans were delightful, were they not?
And who can match our eloquence when high?

FIRST ATHENIAN DELEGATE:
Unless we're sloshed, we don't make any sense!
If the Athenians took my advice,
we'd go on all our foreign missions drunk.   1230
Whenever we arrive in Sparta now,
we look for something to complain about.
We hardly notice what they have to say,
and think that what they haven't said they mean.
So our reports are contradictory.
This feast was perfect. If a Spartan sang
the Telamon and not Cleitagora,[79]
we praised him anyway and even swore . . .

(Slaves are inching their way toward the Acropolis gate.)

Look there! Those slaves are sneaking back again.

(He rises to chase the returning slaves away.)

Get out of here you worthless whipping posts!   1240

(The slaves scatter accompanied by the chorus's laughter.)

79. Drinking songs. Telamon is the name of Ajax the Greater's half-brother; Cleitagora (klā-ta´-gə-rə), of an otherwise unknown woman. It is not known what sort of faux pas the Athenians tolerated.

SECOND ATHENIAN DELEGATE:
Oh look! Some other guests are coming out.

   (The SPARTAN DELEGATES enter. One is playing a
    panpipe.)

SPARTAN DELEGATE (addressing a companion):
Do take these pipes away, my dearest love.
I fain would do the double kick and sing
to honor these Athenians and us.

FIRST ATHENIAN DELEGATE:
Oh yes! By gods! Do take his pipes away!
I love to watch you people sing and dance!

SPARTAN DELEGATE (dancing while singing):
Unto this lad do not refuse
to hasten, Memory, thy Muse,   1250
who having come must not be dumb
but sing of Artemisium,[80]
how men of Athens, even they,
overcame the Medes one day,
while King Leonidas[81] *led us*
like boars become cantankerous.
She'll not forget our feat to fete

---

80. Artemisium (är-tə-miz´-ē-əm), a promontory on the coast of Euboea,
the site of an indecisive three-day sea battle between the Greeks and invading Persians. Fought at the same time as Thermopylae.

81. Leonidas (lē-ä´-nə-dəs), Spartan king and leader of the three hundred
Spartans who fought to the death at Thermopylae.

nor how our jaws with drool were wet,
and say, in truth, the Persian band   1260
far outnumbered grains of sand.
And you beast-killer of the wild,
hie thee hither, undefiled,[82]
ratify our rites of peace
lest our prosperous friendship cease.
All the wily tricks we know
for such a peace we shall forego.   1270
Leader of the canine crowd,[83]
hie thee hither, maiden proud.

 (LYSISTRATA escorts the delegates' wives from the
  Acropolis.)

FIRST ATHENIAN DELEGATE:
Since everything's been taken care of now,
it's time that each of you, Athenians
and Spartans, join your wives and stand beside
each other, man and wife. That done, we'll dance
to celebrate our joy and our resolve
never to do such foolish things again.

 (Singing and dancing like the SPARTAN DELEGATE while
  the chorus claps hands.)

Bring the chorus on!
Also the Graces three!

 82. The goddess Artemis, a virgin huntress.
 83. Artemis again, the leader of hunters and their dogs.

Also Artemis　　　　　　　　　　　　　　　1280
wherever she may be.
Also her friendly sib,
Apollo, healing god.
Also the Maenads' friend,
the lord of Nysa's sod,[84]
the god with flashing eyes,
Bacchius by name.
Also call on Zeus,
and his candescent flame.
And then his blessed wife.
We have to call on both
and all the gods to witness
our ever-mindful oath
that we shall not allow
the memory to fade
of this high-minded peace
that Aphrodite's made.　　　　　　　　　　　1290

UNIFIED CHORUS:
Ala! Alee!
Ala Paean!
Begin the dancing! Eee!
Euvo! Euvo!
Leeoh! Leeoh!
Hurray for winning! Eee!

FIRST ATHENIAN DELEGATE:
Okay, Spartan, now's your turn to match our latest song.

84. Dionysus, who was said to have been raised by nymphs on the (mythical) Mt. Nysa (nī´-sə).

SPARTAN DELEGATE:

Leaving fair Taÿgetus
come hither, Muse of mine,
praise Amyclae's[85] patron and
Athena's brazen shrine,
praise the noble Tyndarids,[86]   1300
often seen beside
the swift Eurotas[87] River where
they frolic in their pride.
Eia mala! Start the dance!
Eia mala O!
Gallop lightly o'er the field
until we holler "Whoa!"
Then celebrate old Sparta's land
where choruses abound
and one can hear their dancing feet,
leveling the ground.
The maidens frisk like colts beside
the swift Eurotas where
the clouds of dust their feet arouse
bedim the summer air.   1310
They whirl their tresses all about
like maenads going wild.

---

85. Amyclae (ə-mī´-klē), a village in Lacedaemon on the eastern bank of the Eurotas a few miles south of Sparta.

86. Tyndarids (tin´-də-rids), children of Tyndareos, king of Sparta and nominal father of Helen, Clytaemestra, Castor, and Pollux, really the offspring of Zeus disguised as a swan.

87. Eurotas (yü-rō´-təs), one of the main rivers of the Peloponnesus, flowing from north to south through Lacedaemon.

Their leader's pure and decorous,
fair Helen, Leda's child.[88]
Now bind your hair and tell your feet
to stomp the meadow floor.
Let your hands clap rhythm while
our choral voices soar
to hymn the goddess housed in bronze,   1320
invincible in war.

---

88. Helen of Sparta, the infamous adulteress but spoken of respectfully by her fellow Spartans.

Appendix 1

The Pronunciation of Unfamiliar Names

Lysistrata contains a large number of proper nouns with which nonclassicist readers may be unfamiliar. I have noted the ones that seemed the most likely to require clarification. Because of the importance I attach to reading aloud, I include phonetic spellings and stress marks for each term.

Classical Greek is thought not to have had stress accents. When Greek words became naturalized in Latin and/or English, they followed the Latin rule for positioning stresses, namely the next-to-last syllable is stressed when it is closed, that is, the vowel is followed by two or more consonants, or the syllable contains a naturally long vowel sound; otherwise, the third-syllable from the end is stressed. Hence we call Artemis "är´-tə-məs," not "är-tē´-məs," but her brother, Apollo, "ə-päl´-lō," not "ä´-pə-lō." Since the first *a* in Lysistrata is a short vowel in an open syllable, she should be called lī-sis´-trə-tä, not lī-sis-trä´-tä. By the same token, her Spartan counterpart is lam´-pə-tō, not lam-pē´-tō. Naturally long, open vowels are less frequent. An example is Athena (ə-thē´-nä).

Symbols Used in Phonetic Spellings

ə: as in the first and last syllable of *America*

a: as in *bat*

ä: as in *father*

ā: as in *say*

e: as in *get*

ē: as in *be*

i: as in *it*

ī: as in *eye*

ō: as in *go*

ȯ: as in *awe*

ü: as in *loose*

To reduce the number of notes needed, here are the names given to individual choristers by their respective leaders. The men: Drakes (drä´-kēz), Philurgus (fi-lər´-gəs), and Phaedrias (fē´-dri-əs); the women: Nikodika (ni-kō´-di-kä), Calyx (kā´-liks), Crytilla (krī-til´-lä), and Rhodippe (rō-dip´-pē).

Appendix 2

Meters Used in Translating Spoken Lines

I have not attempted to imitate the metrical qualities of Aristophanes' choral odes or other musical passages. As in my translations of tragedy, I distinguish lyrical passages by translating them as short, rhymed stanzas (so they sound like songs) and italicizing them. In translating spoken passages, I try to copy the various rhythms of the Greek. The assumption underlying this effort is that long syllables in the Greek line were the functional equivalent of stressed syllables in English.

In describing poetic meters, the Greeks referred to metrons. For our purposes, a metron can be defined as a pair of poetic feet describing the permitted distribution of long, short, and unregulated syllables in a poetic line of a given type. A dash (–) signifies a position that can be occupied by a long syllable, u by a short syllable, and x by an unregulated syllable, the iambic metron is x–u–. An iambic trimeter consists of three iambic metrons.

Iambic trimeter is the meter closest to normal speech and was employed accordingly in both comedy and tragedy. In my translations, I have followed the usual practice of translating Greek iambic trimeters as iambic pentameters in English, for example lines 6–7.

Hello, Lysistrata! You seem upset.
You shouldn't frown. You'll hurt your looks that way.

I have allowed spondees to substitute for iambs in any position and occasionally an initial trochee, for example, line 33:

either the Peloponnesians all must die . . .

Passages Using Iambic Pentameter

1–253: The prologue in which Lysistrata organizes her sex strike.
387–466: The Commissioner tries to arrest Lysistrata.
608–613: The Commissioner and Lysistrata withdraw.
706–780: Lysistrata prevents desertions.
829–952: The Kinesias episode.
980–1013: The Spartan herald and Kinesias.
1074–1107: The Spartan delegation enters.
1112–1187: Lysistrata supervises negotiations.
1216–1247: The Athenian banqueters emerge.
1273–1278: Lysistrata arranges the final procession.

In several meters, the final metron is cut short by a syllable. These verses are called catalectic. During the first half of *Lysistrata*, Aristophanes uses iambic tetrameter catalectic for agitated speech. As its name implies, this meter consists of four iambic metrons with the last syllable missing:

x–u– / x–u– / x–u– /x–x.

Lines in this meter in Greek frequently have a diaeresis (i.e., a momentary pause in the middle where a word ending corresponds to the end of the second metron). In translating, I adhere to the Greek model except that I allow spondees in any position and have a diaeresis in every line, for example 254–255:

Keep marching, Drakes! Lead the way! Ignore your aching
   shoulder!
Don't let that load of olive trunks defeat your manly spirit.

Passages Imitating Iambic
Tetrameter Catalectic

254–255: The Men's Leader urges his choristers to hurry to the Acropolis.

266–270: More exhortation by the Men's Leader.

281–285: The Men's Leader recalls the embarrassment of Cleomenes.

306–318: The Men's Leader coaxing his fire to life.

319–320: The Women's Leader urges her choristers to hurry to the Acropolis.

350–386: After an exchange of threats, the Women's Leader gives the Men's Leader an unwanted bath.

467–475: The Men's Leader and the Women's Leader exchange rebukes.

539–540: The Women's Leader tells her choristers to perform.

Anapestic tetrameter catalectic is a rapid meter used primarily for the lively debate between Lysistrata and the Commissioner. It consists in theory of four anapestic metrons catalectic, reverse dactyls in other words: u u–u u–. There is great variety in actual practice. The two short syllables in each foot may be (and often are) changed to a single long; the long syllable may be changed into two shorts. In adapting this verse, I kept all the short syllables except for allowing an iamb (or even a single long) instead of an anapest in the initial position. I also reduced the length of the line. The Greek tetrameter became an English trimeter, for example 484–485:

Examine her strictly! Dispute every word that she utters!
We cannot approve such an act without knowing its motive.

Passages Imitating Anapestic
Tetrameter Catalectic

484–532: The debate between Lysistrata and the Commissioner.
549–597: The debate continues.
1072–1073: The Men's Leader observes the arrival of the Spartan delegation.
1108–1111: The unified chorus welcomes the return of Lysistrata.

Trochaic tetrameter catalectic is not as rapid as its anapestic counterpart. It is suitable for emphatic statements. It occurs principally in four ten-line speeches by the Men's Leader and the Women's Leader, respectively. Except for allowing spondees in odd-numbered feet, I adhered to the Greek model in translating these lines, for example 614–615:

It's no time for freedom-loving citizens to sleep!
Let's take off our clothing, men, and make these women weep!

Passages Imitating Trochaic Tetrameter Catalectic

614–615: The Men's Leader urges his comrades to strip for action.

626–635: The Men's Leader is angered by women advising men.

636–637: The Women's Leader threatens the Men's Leader.

648–657: The Women's Leader is grateful to the city for various honors.

662–663: The Men's Leader tells his chorus to strip.

671–681: The Men's Leader tell his chorus to beware of women.

689–690: The Women's Leader tells her chorus to strip.

696–705: The Women's Leader denounces the exclusion of Miss Eel from her feast.

1295: An Athenian delegate tells a Spartan that it is time for him to sing.